Praise for Aged Healthy, Wea

"As I approach my 75th birthday, I nave pondered what Erik Erikson meant about the 8th stage of life as Integrity. Covie's book is a gift that answers my question. It has given me a path and way to live integrally. Thank you, Covie."

> — *James (Jay) E. Hughes, Jr., author of* Family Wealth: Keeping it in the Family *and* Family: The Compact Among Generations; *co-author of* The Cycle of the Gift, The Voice of the Rising Generation, *and* Family Trusts

"Just as she did with her first book, Covie takes a positive approach to a topic often riddled with doom and gloom. Read *Aged Healthy, Wealthy & Wise*, and you may actually look forward to your older years as a time of proactive agency and honest self-reflection."

> — *Ryan Ansin, Revolutionary Farms and President of the Family Office Association*

"I've seen firsthand how Covie's pioneering first book has transformed families. Having just finished *Aged Healthy, Wealthy & Wise*, I have no doubt that it will do the same. This is an incredibly important topic, and Covie tackles the issue of aging from the perspective of vibrant older individuals whom all of us, not just those at the later end of life, can learn from. She incorporates stories and helpful tools throughout the book for the reader to use as a guide to help live a vibrant later life and also incorporates valuable information for the family members supporting them. A must-read for all of us at any age!"

> — *Mariann Mihailidis, Managing Director of the Family Office Exchange*

"As our world—and our profession—faces the conundrum of aging, this book provides insights into how to thrive to the end, with wisdom taken from the ultimate experts: the people who are actually doing it in real life."

— *Bob Veres, Editor of* Inside Information

"Peter Drucker once said, 'The most serious mistakes are not being made as a result of wrong answers. The true dangerous thing is asking the wrong question.' Coventry Edwards-Pitt's latest and most impressive undertaking includes a generous helping of insightful and thought-provoking questions. Distilling and compiling the very best of current research and resources, this original take on aging deserves a permanent home in any family's library—and in their advisors', too!"

— *Charlotte B. Beyer, President of the Principle Quest Foundation and Founder of The Institute for Private Investors*

"Covie masterfully weaves together stories of elders in a way that is instructive and inspiring for family members at any age. With so much attention focused on 'the kids' in our society, *Aged Healthy, Wealthy & Wise* offers a refreshing window into the lifelong endeavor of living a life of purpose and meaning; and, in fact, we discover, it is the key to a joyful existence."

— *Danielle Oristian York, Managing Director of 21/64*

"Coventry Edwards-Pitt follows up her successful first book on raising children with wealth by examining the complementary stage of life in *Aged Healthy, Wealthy, & Wise*. Using a similar format of interweaving research literature with compelling narrative examples, she highlights many of the secrets of aging well in our society. Her clever acronym of AGED captures how to feel well and be productive as life winds down from its hectic, driven adult years. Read it and be inspired."

— *James Grubman, PhD, Family wealth consultant and author of* Strangers in Paradise: How Families Adapt to Wealth Across Generations

"Much has been said in our industry about the tsunami of wealth transfer that will occur over the next few decades, but relatively little has been said about the individuals who will be transferring this wealth and what their aging journeys will be like. This book shows this generation how to age well and ensure that their aging process positively rather than negatively impacts their families."

— *Angelo Robles, Founder and Chairman of the Family Office Association*

Aged Healthy, Wealthy & Wise

Aged Healthy, Wealthy & Wise

Lessons from vibrant and inspiring elders on how they designed their later lives

Coventry Edwards-Pitt

Contents

....

SECTION TWO: PLANNING YOUR LATER YEARS SO THAT
YOU PRESERVE YOUR LEGACY AND FAMILY HARMONY

SECTION THREE: TOOLS AND RESOURCES

Acknowledgments

A heartfelt thank you to:

The interviewees—Thank you for your candor and willingness to share your personal stories with me. I am so inspired by the nuggets you shared with me about how you are leading vibrant later lives and trust many will use your words as a guide as they embark on their own aging paths. And to my next-generation interviewees—thank you for sharing your experiences about caring for your elders. Your words are an invaluable reminder of the true gifts we leave our children.

Our clients—Thank you for allowing me to be a part of your lives for all of these years. I can't imagine a more fulfilling career than being given the opportunity to be your thought partner through the joys and challenges of life. It's a wonderful privilege to be able to help you harness your resources to design later lives that are meaningful.

My partners and professional colleagues at Ballentine Partners—It's a joy coming to work and serving families with you. A special thank you to Roy Ballentine for his mentorship over the years and to Roy, Drew McMorrow, and the rest of my partners for believing in the importance of this work and enabling me to dedicate the time to its creation. Thanks specifically to Roy, Drew, Anja Saloranta, Janie Doherty, Kim Emberg, Jennifer Eaton, Monica Parks, and Leah Warren for their thoughtful comments, which have improved this work.

The great minds in our field, whose work and thought leadership informed both this book and our practice—particularly, thank you to the experts who shared their thoughts with me and whom I have quoted in this book: Ellen Goodman, Bob Mauterstock, David O'Neil, Sarah Putnam, Sally Rosenfield, and Susan Turnbull. Also, thank you to Dr. James Grubman, Ph.D., whose 12-year relationship with our firm and thoughtful trainings have immeasurably deepened my understanding of the psychology of wealth, including how aging impacts the clients we serve. Thank you to Janet Simpson Benvenuti (pen name Jan Simpson), Cheryl Holland, and Carolyn McClanahan, whose work with aging clients informed our practice, and to Bob Veres, for ensuring that best ideas are circulated within our profession. Finally, thank you to the Collaborative for Family Flourishing community—I so value knowing all of you and being able to think deeply about how best to do this work. Thank you for gathering and continuing to create a place for us to exchange best ideas and think creatively about how we serve our client families.

Champions—Thank you to all who have been such champions of the first book and who encouraged me to keep writing. Your moral support made a difference and was much appreciated! In particular, a heartfelt thank you to Lorne Adrain, Chris Alaimo, Samantha Anderson, Ryan Ansin, Ron Avni, Andrea Ayres, Charlotte Beyer, Debbie Bing, Emily Bouchard, Aimee Bryant, Scott Byrnes, Tim Cestnick, Joanne Cohen, Susan Colpitts, Jamie Cornell, Jim Coutre, Leigh Davis, Jenni Leisman Dessert,

Jackie Downing, Sid Efromovich, Merav Fine, Ken Foraste, Laura Godine, Sharna Goldseker, Robin and Luba Greenwood, Jill Hagler, Fredda Herz Brown, Hamilton Hilsman, Jay Hughes, Jack Heath, Alice Jacobs, Audrey Jacobs, Joey and Jennifer Kolchinsky, Dori Kreiger, Bill Leisman, Will Leisman, Jo Leonard, Mariann Mihailidis, Suma Nair, Neil Nisker, Arden O'Connor, Ruben Orduña, Ellen Perry, Rama Ramaswamy, Jim Rappaport, Karen Rancourt, Joe Reilly, Chris Rein, Morris and Debbie Robinson, Angelo Robles, Tom Rockwell, Greg Rogers, Carol Rugani, David Salem, Judy Salerno, Myra Salzer, Cathy Schmidt, Barbara Taylor, John A. Warnick, Randy Webb, Deb Wetherby, Jonah Wittkamper, Kim Wright, Danielle York, the 21/64 network of trainers, the wonderful women in my WPO group, and all of the people who have attended my book talks.

Katrin Schumann—Thank you for your insights, sense of humor, encouragement, and belief in this topic. Your work helping me to define and shape the project and find the right words was invaluable.

Janie Doherty—Thank you for your Herculean efforts scheduling countless interviews, managing the book production calendar, and checking references. I truly could not have done this project without your steady assistance day in and day out!

The book production team—Thank you to Kim Emberg for managing the publication process, Ursula DeYoung for copyediting, Kacy Colson for the book's interior design, and Dominic Oliver, Katie Jansen, Jiah Park, Tom Hayes, Maddie Press, Alexander Duckworth, and Elijah Duckworth-Schachter from Point One Percent for their beautiful cover design.

My family—Thank you to my mother, Virginia Edwards, who shows me every day how to age well, with good humor, optimism, adaptability, and drive. To my father, Howard Pitt, whose sense of humor and love of learning continue to inspire me. I wish you had had more years on your aging journey. And to my brother, Celidon Pitt, and sister-in-law, Wynne Kandur, thank you for being there to laugh with, for being such wonderful role models for my daughter, and for all you do to help keep alive the flame of our family memories. Thank you also to my in-laws, Sondra and Charlie Weinzierl, for their presence in our lives and for the many conversations on this topic, which helped shape my thinking.

My husband—Thank you for being a true partner in life and for making it fun.

My daughter—Thank you for all the joy you bring to life and for being so supportive during the book-writing process.

Aged Healthy, Wealthy & Wise

Introduction

We are on the cusp of an unprecedented demographic shift. By 2020, the number of Americans 65 and older will outnumber those under five years of age[1], and by 2060, they will make up nearly a quarter of the population (up from 15% currently and 9% in 1960)[2]. The impact of this change will be felt everywhere.

We see this shift from the perspective of the wealthy families we advise. Over the next decades, many of the clients we have worked with for years will enter what used to be known as "old age" and then live even longer. We will see our middle-aged clients spend more of their time and resources on finding adequate support for their own aging parents. The aging of the baby boomers and the increases in longevity that they are enjoying mean that our role as advisors will increasingly be about helping our clients use their resources to ensure that they and their parents are aging well.

But there's a stumbling block in our way: people resist, even fear, thinking about aging, and, paradoxically, this resistance prevents them from taking the steps that would not only mitigate what they fear but actually enhance their aging experience and make it more fulfilling. Why is this? For one, people rarely think of themselves as old—most feel like an 82-year-old client of mine who told me, laughing, "Inside, I'm still 42 years old!" Second, actually contemplating aging brings up all sorts of thorny issues—health, living arrangements, succession, conflict over estate planning decisions, even death—that are in no one's nature to enjoy contemplating.

We see this dynamic play out in our work. The wealthy families who seek our advice handling their finances expect us to delve into the financial aspects of aging. Questions like "Will my assets be sufficient to support me for the remainder of my life?" and "Should we gift more to a trust to lower our estate-tax burden?" are easy to help our clients answer. There are numbers, graphs, and charts that provide a ready solution. But deeper questions like "Will my children be happy with my estate planning decisions after I'm gone?" or "Where will I find motivation and purpose when I step back from my career?" are harder to answer and often discomfiting for our clients even to consider.

We have found, though, over the course of our work that talking about only the easy questions does not ensure a high quality of life or peace of mind in later years. And more importantly, it does nothing to ensure a good outcome for families who are impacted by a loved one's aging process.

In my role as Chief Wealth Advisory Officer for our firm, I'm charged with thinking deeply about the problems our clients will face and figuring out how we can best help them solve them. That is where this book comes in. In 2014, we published the book *Raised Healthy, Wealthy & Wise: Lessons from successful and grounded inheritors on how they got that way*, which aimed to tackle another significant issue our clients face—whether their wealth will interfere with their children's ability to launch productive and independent lives. Our goal was to focus on success stories, interviewing children who had grown up in wealthy families and went on to become happy, well-adjusted, and productive adults, and share the insights we learned about which parenting messages worked. Since then, I've been speaking around the country to advisors and families, sharing the lessons of the book. I have been moved by how inspiring people have found the positive stories that we showcased and how they have been motivated as a result of these stories to make changes in their own parenting and within their own families.

Our aim with this book is to follow the same success-story format and apply it to another pressing issue that will increasingly impact our clients' quality of life—how to have a fulfilling later life and weather the transitions this period in life inevitably brings with as little family discord, and as much peace of mind, as possible.

What this book adds to the discussion

There is certainly much in the public conversation already about how to prolong health as we get older; we all know to exercise and eat right, and there are many good books explaining how to do that (some of which appear in our recommended reading list in the appendices). Our goal was to focus on the more intangible aspects of aging that contribute to a vibrant later life and show, through concrete positive examples, how people are living these factors in their own lives. We wanted to know, what are people who are feeling vibrant and youthful as they age doing to help them feel that way?

The first section of the book details the four success factors that we observed throughout our many discussions, brought to life by the real stories of our interviewees. Those factors are:

- Agency
- Growth
- Engagement with others
- Drive

You will notice that these four factors also happen to match the acronym AGED. To be clear, we didn't start with the letters and then find the factors! But an amazing thing happened—once we did the interviews and the factors began to emerge, it was clear that these four were the most important and that they could be described, both in name and in order, by the acronym AGED. This is serendipitous, but serves a purpose. First, we hope it makes these four characteristics memorable so that they serve as an inspiring reminder to anyone embarking on the daily work of organizing a later life. Second, we hope that it helps put an end to the sometimes negative connotation that the word AGED carries and infuses it with the wisdom, energy, and aspiration that this phase of life represents and affords. Wouldn't it be wonderful if we all could think, "Yes, I want to be AGED!"

In the second section, we turn to a subject that almost every single one of our interviewees found somewhat intimidating: preparing for the last years of life and the end-of-life process. We aim to show that one of the best gifts we can give our loved ones is a well-thought-out and articulated plan for this stage of life. While it is a subject no one likes to talk about, we will show that facing reality does not have to be frightening, and can actually be incredibly empowering for everyone involved.

As part of this section, we look at the power of sharing family stories as a way to continue contributing once you're gone, and we show that communicating the meaning behind your estate planning decisions is a powerful way to articulate your values and avoid confusion and bitterness after your passing. We highlight stories from interviewees about loved ones who proactively addressed dementia or dying and the grateful families who felt they were given a lasting gift as a result. Finally, we provide a number of critical questions for you to think through so that you too can give your family the gift of thinking clearly and transparently about this stage of your life. In all, we aim to leave readers with a comprehensive handbook of all that it takes to age well and to allow your aging to positively (rather than negatively) impact your family.

Taking control

Certainly, as we age, some things will be out of our control, such as whether we develop dementia or cancer, or encounter other physical or mental limitations. But this book is about what we can control: namely the type of life we strive to lead as we age. Will we embrace a sense of agency or allow our days to play out passively? Will we choose to see change as a way to grow and learn? Will we do the work required to stay engaged with the larger world and maintain a sense of purpose? Will we stumble into the end of life and leave choices to our children, or will we help them by letting them know what we want? We control our responses to each of these questions, and our responses have a significant impact not only on our own quality of life as we age, but also on the effect our aging process has on our loved ones.

Even with aspects we cannot control, there is much we can

control about how we approach these areas and much good that can come from owning our ability to author how we face them. Part of what stymies people is that they resist the things they can't control about aging (wrinkling skin, declining physical ability), while avoiding the things they do have the ability to control— things that would have tremendous positive impact on their loved ones. For example: recording their wishes for their dying process, proactively designing a succession plan for their family enterprise, or writing an ethical will that will demonstrate the meaning to their loved ones behind the financial inheritance they will receive.

Throughout, we share stories we heard from our interviewees about how either they or a loved one found the courage to face these issues head on, and how meaningful this decision ended up being for their families. Our hope is that the stories of people who have tackled these issues positively will inspire you to take these steps in your own life and with your own family.

Our research process

We conducted many different types of interviews, with older clients and non-clients, with their children, and with consultants. We chose to interview older people whom we wanted to emulate—who seem to be living content, full lives, and who we all would "want to be" when we get older. Our older interviewees were split evenly into groups of equal size in their 60s, 70s, and 80s. We were able to access in our discussions with these interviewees not only their own experiences, but also the wisdom and stories they could share from having watched their own parents or friends go through the aging process. In some instances, our interviewees could almost time-travel and speak from the perspective of both the elder they are now and the child they once were, remembering inspiring older relatives they knew 60 or 70 years ago. In all, we accessed shared memory and history going back over 150 years.

It truly was a gift to be able to hear our interviewees' stories and learn about their lives. Sadly, our society does not make it easy to spend time accessing the wisdom of our elders. It was wonderful to have a chance to talk with these fascinating individuals and hear their advice on how to lead a fulfilling life. Now, a number of months on from these discussions, I find that their wisdom sticks with me, and I often notice myself calling to mind a story they shared when I'm looking for a little inspiration in my day. I hope you will discover in reading the book that these stories do the same for you.

We heard in a number of our conversations that our interviewees were moved by our discussion and found the process of thinking through the questions enlightening; many told us that our discussion inspired them to share these questions and their thoughts with their spouses and children. As a result, we included the list of questions we asked our interviewees in the appendix of this book, so perhaps you might contemplate them yourself. As in the last book, we have changed names and some details in order to protect the anonymity of our interviewees; but, we have kept all of their quotes verbatim, so you can hear their voices as we did.

In addition to the interviews we conducted, we also acquainted ourselves with the copious literature and research currently available on aging. We have highlighted the most salient points from the many valuable books and articles we read (all are incorporated in the endnotes), and we have included the resources we found most helpful in a recommended reading list at the end.

Who is this book for?

This book is for anyone who wonders about how best to use their resources to maximize their quality of life as they age. We summarize what we heard from our interviewees about the factors that have enabled them to have fulfilling later-life experiences and show how they have leveraged their resources to cultivate these factors. We also focus on the intersection of aging and financial resources, delving into questions like "If you have the resources to age well, how do you optimally use them? How should you invest your time and money to design a life that will enhance your ability to age well? And what planning should you do now to maximize your chances that the resources you leave behind will positively rather than negatively impact your family after you're gone?"

While this book is about aging, it is not just for people currently at a later stage in their lives—it is also for their children. How often have we heard from friends or colleagues whose parents' later-life experiences proved to be terrifying, exhausting, financially draining, or confusing for their children? All too frequently, the impulse is to wait another day before facing the reality of aging; we tend to underestimate the importance of clearly stating our wishes and planning ahead to make sure our wishes can be carried out without causing conflict or pain in our families. This avoidance leaves the younger generation holding the full burden of responsibility for making choices in times of extreme stress. Our hope is that an adult child in the throes of helping an aging parent might be buoyed by these stories and may find in this book the resources necessary either to help make their situation more manageable or inspire their parent to action that would positively impact their family.

Sharing accumulated wisdom

Our work with client families over the last 30 years has given us the opportunity to shepherd a number of clients through the aging process. We have seen what type of later-life planning promotes family harmony, and what kinds of mistakes sow discord for multiple generations, despite best intentions. Our aim with this book is to go beyond the standard advice to get deeper, to really dig into the practical steps that you can and should take today to improve not only your own aging process but also the effect that your aging will have on your loved ones.

We intentionally tackle the topic from a variety of perspectives, as that is how we all experience aging ourselves. Each of us is both on our own aging journey and is likely at some point to be helping a loved one at a later stage of life. In that vein, we showcase both the reflections and insights of our older interviewees on what has enabled them to live fulfilling lives, as well as the voices of adult children in mid-life as they identify the actions their parents have taken that they have found particularly inspiring or helpful. We heard poignant, beautiful stories from many grown children about how a parent modeled grace and joy in the face of declining abilities or provided invaluable clarity by articulating his or her wishes about death. We found this perspective particularly instructive because we heard from most of our older interviewees how much they hoped they would not be a burden on their children; the voices of these children and the concrete examples they provide show us all how not to be.

We are also mindful that this is a topic many of us live every day. I've seen this personally myself—in the time that I have worked on this book, I have been a caregiver to a family member with cognitive difficulties, have helped a relative move to a senior living community, and have hired many of the consultants in the panoply of eldercare (from geriatric care managers, to move managers, to doctors of all stripes) to assist with both. It is certainly an education, and what we all learn going through this process is that we are not alone. We all struggle with how to do this well— both in our own lives and in trying to help our aging loved ones. We hope this book will give you a roadmap to turn to if you find yourself on this path.

Since aging is not necessarily a given, experiencing old age can be seen as a kind of gift. This book will help you make the most of that gift, by helping you to acknowledge mortality, manage it the best that you can, and design a later life that will enable you and your loved ones to thrive.

SECTION ONE

Chapter One
Agency

....

Owning Your Role as the Author of Your Own Experience

In the course of our research, we were startled by the number of our interviewees who expressed a surprisingly similar sentiment: you have to make your own life—no one else will do it for you. There was a real sense of proactive, capable authorship, and an absence of passive victimhood. We started to hear this idea in various incarnations frequently enough that it became clear that it was foundational—that, in a sense, all of the other lessons our interviewees shared with us stemmed from this attitude, this proactive posture and conviction that they had the ability (and responsibility) to make their lives what they wanted them to be.

We decided "agency" is the best way to describe and refer to this attitude. In sociology and philosophy, agency is the capacity of a person—or an entity—to act. This may sound simple, yet many people operate without a sense of agency, either because they do not have the will or courage to act or because they feel they are being held back by something beyond their control. The author Salman Rushdie finds the issue of human agency a constant preoccupation. "The question I'm always asking myself is: are we masters or victims?" he told *The Times* of London in 2008.[3] "The question of do we have agency in our lives or whether we are just passive victims of events is, I think, a great question."

Though Rushdie asks this question while exploring cultural and religious landscapes as a novelist, it is no less important to ask ourselves the same question: As we age, will we seek to be active architects and builders of our own experiences? Are we firmly in charge of our lives and our happiness, or do we allow life to happen to us?

Margo, age 81 and a former biology teacher from Long Island, is determined not to let fear or uncertainty stop her from being in charge. Though she considers herself an introvert, she proudly declares that she makes a conscious effort to put herself out into the world, rather than give in to her innate reticence. A favorite part of her routine had been taking an early morning train from her Connecticut home into New York City, getting on the subway to cross town, and walking through a tunnel and up three flights of stairs—all the while lugging supplies—to reach an art class she had signed up for. However, in recent months, Margo's back has been giving her trouble and she finds that the long trip into the city is too much. But, rather than dwelling on what she cannot do, Margo is matter of fact and focused on what she chooses to embrace next. She jokes that it's time to take up bridge, and then says, "You have to keep busy. You have to make your own life. No one will do it for you…You do what you have to do. Make lemonade. That's it."

As another interviewee, Helen, also in her 80s, put it: "You've got to make yourself a human being who wants to do things…

You just have to keep going. You can't sit around and feel sorry for yourself."

The power of role models

We learned that it is easier for people to embrace agency in their later years when they have inspiring role models to remember and emulate. Margo told us about her grandmother, who washed the tile floors of her home on her hands and knees at 90 and who generally displayed a robustness and can-do attitude that kept her consistently lively and engaged. Margo was also moved by another relative, Millie, who lived beyond 100 and whose philosophy of life was to enjoy each and every minute. Each day she would get dressed, put on her makeup, go out to eat, and play Mahjong. "She used to say 'Don't worry about everything; things will work out.'" Margo explained. Even though her husband had died young, Millie lived happily into old age, letting her positive attitude guide her.

Our interviewee Helen, who spent many decades managing the real-estate company she had built while raising her four children, talked fondly about her own mother, Agnes, who was originally from the south of France. As a child, Agnes loved to swim, surf, and run, and she has always been physically active. At age 105, Agnes now lives in an assisted-living community and is extremely independent. She attends lectures, is always practicing her German and French, walks a mile a day, and has a number of friends who keep her busy. "I'm not hovering over her," Helen said. "She would drive me crazy, and I would drive her crazy!" Joking aside, Helen deeply admires the life her mother has carved out for herself—she is self-possessed, interesting, optimistic, and self-sufficient—and is a remarkable role model to her family and others.

Our interviewee, Peggy, told us the story of her closest aunt's significant other, Charlie. Peggy's aunt was widowed in middle age and several years later met Charlie, who became her companion until her own death 30 years later. Charlie became close with Peggy's large family and almost like an uncle to Peggy. Now, in her mid-60s, when Peggy considers how she wants to enter into the later stages of her life, her thoughts go to Charlie and to the example he set in his last decades.

Charlie loved theater and music, and he was interested in politics and current events. But, more than that, he seemed genuinely interested in others. He would ask people about themselves and seemed intent on learning about others' perspectives. "He was so interested and interesting, and people adored him," Peggy told us. When Charlie turned 90, Peggy's family and a big group of friends threw a birthday party for him; Peggy's siblings, their spouses, and their children came from as far as Montana and Florida to celebrate together, even though Charlie was not actually a blood relative. "Just the fact that they all wanted to be here for his birthday is a reflection of what a nice person he was, and how engaged he was," Peggy explained. She and her family remained close to Charlie right up until his death at age 94. "I want to age in a way that people still want to be around me," Peggy told us, reflecting on Charlie's charisma. "I don't want to be one of those people [who] is always cranky."

When passivity takes over

Although we're committed in this book, as in the last one, to focusing on positive stories, it is sometimes equally powerful to share examples of what not to do. Our discussions with our interviewees made it clear that they were influenced by these types of counterexamples when they encountered them in their own lives.

In particular, most of the people we interviewed had a clear goal of not wanting to be a burden for their children as they aged. For some, this commitment was forged in their own experience of having been on the receiving end of a situation that was, euphemisms aside, quite burdensome. We want to share what we heard from our interviewees about these situations, as these stories inform the commitment to agency and proactivity that many of our interviewees developed as a result.

Our interviewee Karen has had a difficult experience dealing with her aging mother. Karen grew up near Philadelphia with three brothers and a sister; her father was a scientist, and her mother, Sofia, stayed at home with the children. Originally from Spain, Sofia still has long, jet-black hair and a forceful personality at age 91. Life with her is not always easy. "My mom is one of my biggest challenges," Karen told us, before admitting with some hesitation that her mother is narcissistic and can be quite mean and difficult. "She is very extreme, very selfish... It's just not a positive relationship for me."

Now living in North Carolina, Karen says that she tries to be the "dutiful daughter," calling her mother in Philadelphia once a week and visiting every few months. "I try to be really positive with her, but it's very difficult and stressful," Karen explained. Karen leaves these calls and visits, which are fraught with tension, feeling sad and guilty. Sofia makes no effort to form friendships in her community and complains all the time that she is bored. "There's only so much you can do for someone," Karen said when considering her mother's lack of initiative. She seemed both re-signed and wistful as she spoke. "People need to help themselves. It's hard if you're not willing."

When Karen looks toward her own future, she resolves to be different around her own children. "I don't want to be perceived as difficult, selfish, where it's all about me," she says. "I want my children to want to be around me."

Behavior is a choice

Naturally, no one ages with the intention of being a burden on his or her children; certainly, Karen's mother does not con-sciously choose to be difficult. But not choosing to act creates its own set of problems and its own negative reverberations.

Jean and George have been married for 32 years and have lived near Detroit for decades. George, a tall man with a runner's physique, spent his career in engineering and retired early, at age 51. Jean raised their three children then returned to school to become a bookkeeper. She is adventurous and crafty, and quick to laugh. In separate conversations with both of them, they quickly turned to a discussion of their respective mothers, and the impact their mothers' contrasting approaches to aging have had on their own attitudes toward getting older.

"You can choose to be involved in life and be enthused by life, and it's just such a healthy thing to do," Jean explained—yet her own mother does not approach life this way. She calls often to grumble about things, such as when the lawn isn't mowed to her satisfaction or the refrigerator is broken. Her aches and pains are dominant topics of conversation. As a consequence, every inter-action feels like an obligation and a burden. "She's a fairly needy and negative person. What I've learned is that I don't want to be like that. I don't want to constantly call my children and demand this and that," Jean said.

In stark contrast, her husband George's mother never complains and "by not complaining, her needs seem to be met better," Jean said. She has a sense of humor, is empathetic, and is a conversationalist who tells stories and jokes. She considers everyone she meets a friend. "She has such a joy for life and makes the best out of bad situations. And she has had a hard life," Jean said. "She rolls with the punches. She always smiles—you feel the inner peace and joy come out of her."

When we hand over responsibility for our happiness to others, we end up losing out. Henry had a loving and easygoing relationship with both his parents, but when his father died, things changed. It seemed best to have his mother, Evelyn, who was 67 at the time, move in with Henry's sister in Connecticut. There she could live in a spare room on the ground floor that offered privacy and even a small kitchenette.

Before long, Evelyn had become entirely dependent on her daughter for all her social interactions. She did not cultivate any friends of her own. It was not long before this led a resentment to build up: though entirely devoted to her children and grandchildren, Evelyn felt she could never get enough attention from them. This problem has only worsened over time. Henry calls her two or three times a week, yet Evelyn still feels slighted, complaining that New York City Mayor Bloomberg manages to call his mother every single day, despite running an entire city. "I think it's somewhat selfish of parents—it's almost like they feel like they're owed this [attention]," Henry said.

Evelyn is a sweet and generous woman who has lost her

sense of agency. Henry added that his mother's life has become so narrow that they even have problems holding interesting conversations now. "You have to stay vital and interesting, otherwise people will treat you like a museum piece," he said. "They'll respect you and love you, but you won't be impactful in their lives."

Henry and his wife have taken this experience to heart and have decided that with their own children, they want to be the "easy parents." Both were previously married, so their adult children have a choice about whom they want to visit on weekends or holidays—and Henry hopes they will want to visit him. "If you want to come and visit us, you're welcome any time. If you don't want to come and visit us, there's no guilt," he said.

He summarizes his attitude this way: "I just don't want to be a crotchety old person... I don't think anybody wants to be that way, but they end up there. It's about maintaining self-awareness around that. It requires action not to be a burden."

A call to action

Sometimes as people get older, they become aware of a lack of agency in their lives that undermines what could otherwise be a content and healthy existence. When our interviewee Diane was in her mid-40s, she felt that her life was drifting along haphazardly. Her friends all seemed to be in crisis or on the verge of divorce. She too worried that her life had no solid foundation: she had left the work world when her children, now pre-teens, were born, and she felt insecure about her lack of work experience or marketable skills. A deeply shy and cautious person, Diane could not even bring herself to drive the four hours it would take to attend a friend's funeral alone. She was not adventurous and depended on her husband to make almost all decisions. As the marriages around her were crumbling, she began questioning her own life. "I found myself very unhappy, and I needed to do something—and I didn't know what that was," she said. "I felt like I wasn't interesting. I was bored with myself."

One day, she came to a realization that ended up changing her life in ways she could never have foreseen. Her husband, Jim, is an Australian who traveled extensively in his younger days—living variously in Europe, Asia, and South Africa. In middle age, Jim had become more of a homebody: he was committed to work, where he put in long hours, and no longer felt the pull toward adventure. One afternoon, as Diane was driving to pick up one of her children from school and musing about her life, she began thinking about France and about how much she would love to go to Paris. She was remembering that Jim had once told her that as far as he was concerned, he had already been to Paris and did not plan to go back.

Sitting in her car, Diane had a sudden, alarming insight: "He will never take me to Paris." And if he didn't take her, did that mean she would never go? This led her to ask herself some serious questions. "Who am I? What does that mean? What do I do?" Diane explained. "After that, I did not look to anyone to make me happy; I started my journey inward."

How did she take control of her life? "I got a voice," she said. "When you do things for yourself, the world opens up. You just have to trust it. You have to create the life you want. It doesn't just happen for you." Now, almost 15 years later, her life has changed so much as to be almost unrecognizable—and she is still happily married.

Diane began by returning to school, and then negotiating an

arrangement with her husband in which she was given her own money to do with what she pleased. What she chose to do was travel. Alone. For her first trip, she took a museum tour of Paris, becoming fascinated with art history (she would later become a docent at a prominent fine arts museum). She now travels to a new country each year, has met friends on these trips from all over the world, and has parlayed her newfound sense of agency into a busy social-work practice and a side job helping to manage an active nonprofit that builds schools halfway around the world. "[I]t gives you fuel," she said. "Once you open the door to life, it comes."

"People want to be around me more because I'm happy, not resentful or guilty," she added. And her happiness has inspired others. Her husband has changed his mind about traveling and now asks to join her on some of her trips, and her daughter admires the way her mom took charge of her life. Diane calls the approach to life she discovered a "sacred selfishness," in which she determines what she needs to do to make herself happy and then finds a way to make it happen. She forged a life for herself that is separate from her identity as a mother and wife, and it all began with a change in her mindset.

We are what we think

A growing body of research has emerged substantiating the powerful impact that altering your mindset can have not only on your own satisfaction in life and your impact on others, but also, amazingly, on the way in which you experience aging.

Dr. Ellen Langer, a social psychologist and professor at Harvard University, says that our experiences are formed by the words and ideas we attach to them, and when we live life mindfully we can have a direct impact on those experiences. "Mindful thinking" is when people consistently take in their environment and make proactive choices about how to frame those experiences. In her nearly 40 years of conducting research on this topic, Dr. Langer has discovered a direct correlation between one's mindset and health, revealing that it is possible to become physiologically younger through a changed frame of mind.

In one study, conducted in 1981 and recently detailed in *The New York Times*,[4] Langer invited men in their 70s to a week-long retreat during which they lived as though it were still the 1950s. Their environment, conversations, and activities all scrupulously mimicked the way they had lived 22 years earlier. The appliances were from the '50s, the radio played rock 'n roll, and the conversations were steered toward events from that era. Before arriving, the men were photographed and assessed on measures such as cognition, dexterity, flexibility, hearing, and vision.

After their time-warp experience, each of the men was thoroughly tested once again. It was discovered they had become physically more supple, showed greater manual dexterity, and even sat up taller. Their hearing and eyesight had improved—and independent judges thought they even looked younger. When these men put their minds in an earlier time, according to Langer, their bodies followed suit.

Interestingly, it seemed to matter *how* the men put their minds in an earlier time. Langer ran a control group of another group of men who were put through the same experience except for one thing: they were instructed to reminisce about the past, rather than try to inhabit it. They spoke about their younger selves in the past tense, and the biographies they provided were written in the past tense, with pictures of how they looked currently versus how they looked 20 years younger. While both groups experienced some benefits—the men in both seemed to respond well to spending time in an environment where they were treated as capable, functioning, independent adults—the benefits to the group that tried to mentally inhabit the past were much greater. In particular, they showed greater improvement on joint flexibility, finger length (due to arthritis diminishing), and manual dexterity, and exhibited a 43% increase over the control group in the number of participants who improved on intelligence tests.[5]

The study has been repeated a handful of times with similar results. It was even the theme of a popular British reality TV show broadcast in 2010 called *The Young Ones*. The stunning implications of the results are ones that Dr. Langer has seen echoed in much of the work she and others have done since then, which in a variety of forms has shown that people's behavior and biology are influenced by how they mentally frame an experience—whether they do so consciously or unconsciously.

In her book *Counterclockwise: Mindful Health and the Power of Possibility*,[6] Dr. Langer details another fascinating study in which psychologists had subjects solve anagrams without knowing that the anagrams had been constructed from words stereotypically associated with old age (e.g. "felorguft" from "forgetful"). The control group was provided anagrams from words not associated with aging. After solving the anagrams, the subjects were told they were free to go and, without their knowledge, were timed on their walk to the elevator. The people who had been primed to have a subconscious mental image in their mind of old age walked to the elevator more slowly (or in a more stereotypically "old" way) than those who had not been primed to think of age.

Through these studies and others like them, Dr. Langer has concluded that if people can learn to be mindful, to understand the way in which they perceive their experiences and frame their own self-image in more youthful terms, they can significantly improve both their health and their aging experience.

A best-selling series of books, *Younger Next Year* by Chris Crowley and Henry S. Lodge, supports this view, claiming that we have the ability to control the pace at which we age and that 50% of age-related diseases are preventable through lifestyle changes, most notably exercise. The authors write in one of the books: "Most of what we call aging, and most of what we dread about getting older, is actually decay. That's critically important because we are stuck with real aging, but decay is optional."[7] No one is entirely immune from bad luck or normal biological aging (like graying hair or wrinkling skin), but if aging is not going well, "it may be because you passively let aging happen to you," write the authors. "The energy that comes from a fit body—the cognitive energy, the emotional energy, the optimism—is a powerful surge of goodness in your life as you navigate these years."[8]

Since these and other books explain in great detail the benefits of keeping our bodies active and the specifics of how to do so effectively, we won't go into that here; suffice it to say that our interviewees were clear about the benefits of staying in the game, both physically and mentally.

When limitations come knocking

It's clear that there is much we can control about aging, both mentally and physically, and that agency is the means by which we exert this control. But what happens when we are confronted with changes truly beyond our control? How do we employ agency to effectively manage these changes and still retain the ability to author our own experience? We asked our interviewees how they addressed the times when life threw them a curveball.

Three years ago, when Joseph—father of three and grandfather of seven, who now lives part-time in Palm Springs—first began to suffer bone pain while engaging in vigorous activities, he ignored it. He had always had the habit of planning for the future and being proactive, but the idea of a deteriorating body intimidated him: it was something for which he did not want to plan. But as Joseph was forced to curtail his activities, avoiding the doctor was no longer possible. It was time for a hip replacement. The doctor assured him that post surgery, his intermittent back pain would go away and he could take up more robust physical activities again. But there was work to be done: to endure the operation and ensure a rapid recovery, Joseph first had to lose 30 pounds.

This involved five months of workouts, including weight-lifting and Pilates. He had to watch what he ate and cut out drinking. Once Joseph faced his new reality—realizing that living without this operation would render him immobile and in constant pain—he decided to fully embrace the challenges of becoming healthier and trimmer. The operation was a success, and he decided to continue the lifestyle. He is now in exceptionally good shape and feels better and more energetic than ever before.

"I like feeling the way I do physically," he said. "I like having a healthy body." Instead of seeing the physical setback as a depressing sign of an aging body, he decided to see it as an opportunity, and turned it into a positive experience.

Some of our interviewees who were the most committed to

proactively approaching any limitations they faced were spurred on by the experience of having watched the difficult aging process of parents or friends who had done just the opposite. Our interviewees saw first-hand the problems caused by a passive approach—from not accepting help when needed, to becoming overly dependent on others, to (conversely) being in denial about limitations—and had made up their minds to make choices to live differently.

My colleague Leah Warren shared the story of her great-grandparents' difficult decline and the galvanizing effect that their failure to plan for their aging had on her grandparents, who committed themselves to doing things differently in their own lives. Leah's great-grandparents did not plan for later life, and as a result their aging was exceptionally difficult for everyone. Though cruelty had not previously been in her nature, Leah's great-grandmother's personality shifted when she began suffering from dementia. Leah's father remembers seeing his grandmother strike his mother in the face when he was a little boy of four or five. The task of caring for Leah's great-grandmother as she aged fell largely on Leah's grandmother, Grace, who was also the primary caregiver for four young children at the time and working overnight shifts as a hospital nurse. As a result of these experiences and others, Grace and her husband were determined to be intentional about their own aging, with the goal of taking as many steps as possible to ease the burden on their children and grandchildren.

One of these struck us as particularly ingenious. Every year Leah's grandfather, Bud, voluntarily makes an appointment to assess his ability to continue to drive. He wants to make certain that he retains the cognitive and visual capacity needed to drive safely. In doing this, he has taken the responsibility for deciding when it is time to call it quits out of his daughter's hands and accepted this transition as his own responsibility.

Imagine if everyone approached this situation the way Bud does—how many hurt feelings and intense family struggles might be avoided. The self-awareness he demonstrates, as well as the strength and fortitude to face whatever may come, is a gift to his children and grandchildren, a gift that not only helps maintain family harmony but also offers a positive, confident, and proactive role model of aging for many generations to come.

Agency's mental toolkit

So, if our interviewees displayed an ability to be in charge of their own lives and happiness, how did they do it? What mental tools did they use? Across our discussions, through stories that were funny, inspiring, and poignant, several themes emerged. Below are the four mental tools our interviewees relied on most frequently to help them maintain a mindful, proactive approach to aging:

- Perspective
- Positive attitude
- Gratitude
- Humor

We'll take these one at a time and share with you what we heard from our interviewees as well as studies that show our interviewees are onto something.

PERSPECTIVE IS KEY

Diane, who changed her life when she chose to begin traveling alone, was sitting in the office in the social-work practice she began after finishing her studies. Her brown hair was in a curly halo around her fine-boned face, which was suddenly serious.

She had been talking about how much she loved pursuing the opportunities that had opened up to her once she chose to author her own life. Then she began explaining that she suffers from rheumatoid arthritis, a serious and debilitating disease. In her 30s, she had begun to think of her life in terms of the limitations she struggled against, knowing they would only get worse as she aged. After giving birth to a healthy boy and girl, she would have liked to have a third child but was advised against it because of the symptoms of her illness. She was feeling sorry for herself— until she emerged from her doctor's office and caught sight of a 12-year-old girl who was badly disfigured by the disease.

At that moment, not only was Diane hit with the realization that her symptoms were mild compared to the child's but also, she felt a rush of gratitude that, as a mother, she was the one suffering with the disease rather than one of her children; had it been her daughter who was afflicted, Diane would have been praying for it to have been her instead. Now she thought to herself, "Yes, I'm so grateful I don't have to pray for that. It's me! It's me!"

"I had a real epiphany," she said, running a hand through her curls. "I said, 'Okay it's time to move on. I'm the luckiest person in the world.'"

We heard similar stories from other interviewees. There was a sense of perspective that came from understanding the full spectrum of potential outcomes and realizing that their situation was not the worst on the spectrum; and this perspective gave them the ability to weather difficult moments. For instance, medical ailments seemed less taxing when the alternative was considered. "Okay, I'm around," was a sentiment we often heard.

In *Tuesdays with Morrie*,[9] Mitch Albom marvels over how his former professor, Morrie Schwartz, is able to take a similar approach, even in the midst of suffering from ALS with only a few months to live:

"Dying," Morrie suddenly said, "is only one thing to be sad over, Mitch. Living unhappily is something else. So many of the people who come to visit me are unhappy."

Why?

"Well, for one thing, the culture we have does not make people feel good about themselves. We're teaching the wrong things. And you have to be strong enough to say if the culture doesn't work, don't buy it. Create your own. Most people can't do it. They're more unhappy than me—even in my current condition."

"I may be dying, but I am surrounded by loving, caring souls. How many people can say that?"

POSITIVE ATTITUDE

We're all familiar with the notion that our attitudes and perspectives shape our experiences. Viktor Frankl, a neurologist and psychiatrist imprisoned in a Nazi concentration camp during World War II, wrote of observing prisoners who managed to survive the horror psychologically intact: "Everything can be taken from a man or a woman but one thing: the last of human freedoms to choose one's attitude in any given set of circumstances."[10] He was stunned by humans' ability to weather even the greatest difficulty through the power of their own frame of mind, rather than allowing despair to pervade.

Jean, whose mother-in-law radiates positivity, emphasized to us in her interview the importance of focusing on what's going well. "Even if we go through a stressful aging process, we should always appreciate the good things and minimize the bad things," she said. As another of our interviewees, Judy, put it, "What makes people hurt is not what you have but what you think you don't have."

The good news is, when we choose to see the glass as half full, life becomes easier and more pleasant for us and for others—and we measurably improve our health. A 2002 study from Yale, aptly titled *Longevity Increased by Positive Self-Perceptions of Aging*,[11] revealed striking results about the correlation between attitude and well-being: those with more positive self-perceptions of aging, measured up to 23 years earlier based on how much they disagreed with statements like "As you get older, you are less useful," lived seven and a half years longer than those with less positive perceptions. According to the researchers, after controlling for a variety of factors, the findings suggest, "self-perceptions of aging have an impact on survival…that is far greater than the impact of some other variables that have been previously linked to survival, including gender, socioeconomic status, functional health, and loneliness."

Jean summarized it best: "The one thing we can define for ourselves is having a positive attitude—if you have a positive attitude, everything looks a little better."

But is this really enough? In the 1970s, research[12] revealed that expressed attitudes (such as "I believe exercise is important for your health") did not necessarily lead to change in behavior (e.g., getting off the couch and going for a run). In other words, having a good attitude about something did not automatically lead to improved outcomes—an element of will was still needed in order to translate internal thoughts into external action.

In addition, our environment—social pressure—influences both attitude and action.

If we surround ourselves with people who share certain values and behaviors, we will naturally measure ourselves against and develop our habits in the context of those outside criteria (we'll look at the issue of engagement in greater detail in Chapter Three). After seeing her mother's struggles, our interviewee Karen believes fervently that we can and should control our environment too. "Life is what you make of it," she said. "Put yourself around positive-minded people. Read positive things. Get out and do positive things." Jean also felt this way. "Surrounding yourself with upbeat people—not people who moan and groan—is a very important factor as you get older," she said. "And always having something in front of you that you are looking forward to."

Gratitude

Being mindful of the good things in life and expressing gratitude about them also seems to have a noticeably positive effect on the psychology of aging. Judy is a 73-year-old who came to our interview with blue nails and an attractive outfit accentuated with a wide leather belt. In response to our question "What are your greatest joys day to day?" she hesitated for a moment, then smiled and said, "I can have a great day if I'm feeling well, the sun is out, I'm awake and aware, nothing hurts. Joy is serendipitous; it's good to be alert to things going right."

Helen—the real-estate entrepreneur with the 105-year-old mother—said in answer to the same question, "For instance, today was the first sunny day in weeks; it's a dumb thing, but you get so much pleasure out of a simple walk." Lawrence, an investment banker from San Francisco, feels similarly. He answered this way: "Waking up every morning looking forward to a new day; going to bed each night thankful for another day."

A recent article in *Forbes* detailed a number of scientific studies demonstrating the potential benefits of gratitude across various aspects of life, including physical health, psychological health, and mental resilience. Gratitude for the small and simple things actually leads to action which, the studies argue, in turn improves people's lives in a variety of important ways. One of the studies, published in *Personality and Individual Differences* in 2012, shows not only that grateful people report feeling healthier than other people, but also that grateful people "exercise more often and are more likely to attend regular check-ups with their doctors, which is likely to contribute to further longevity."[13]

HUMOR

We also learned that having a good sense of humor and the ability to laugh at oneself is a helpful antidote to the indignities of aging. Jack, a handsome man in his early 80s who founded a business in the New York area, gestured animatedly as he told us about his various antics in the heyday of his career and beyond. He chuckled continuously as he talked about the ups and downs of his business life; even the sharp turns in the road seemed to be part of one big adventure.

When Margo talked about her various forays into new hobbies, she smiled widely as though laughing at her own ineptitude. "My interests are really very broad," she said, explaining what compelled her to pick up a paintbrush for the first time in her life. "I cannot draw anything, but I said, 'What have I got to lose?'"

Her laughter rang out as she added, "And I actually produced something I think is fabulous!" The interview then devolved into giggles on both sides as she told us of a recent misadventure at her local ShopRite when she apparently caught the eye of a young 60-year-old. He pursued her to the car and asked for a date. "Are you crazy?" she said to him. "I could be your mother!" She said it has always helped her not to take herself too seriously.

Growing up in the mountains of Colorado, our interviewee Lawrence was deeply impacted by his father, Conrad, and by how he approached his life and later years. Conrad was the principal of a boarding school, a man with broad shoulders who always carried himself with authority. He might have appeared intimidating, but he attracted people of all ages to him, even teenagers. Conrad showed appreciation for others, was good at laughing at himself, and, as Lawrence said, was "universally revered by all," students and faculty alike. In the evenings, Conrad's cottage would fill up with people who wanted to just hang out with him. They would laugh uproariously at his entertaining stories, and when he would philosophize about what it means to live a good life, "people ate it up," his son said. "One of the many things about him that impressed me," Lawrence said, "was how he remained engaged with young people as he aged. They sought him out for his wisdom, wit, and wacky sense of humor."

Tapping into his sense of humor and applying it creatively allowed Conrad to have fun throughout his later years. Lawrence remembers how his father made sure that homecomings from high school or college were never boring affairs for Lawrence or his siblings. Engrossed by the humor and challenge in it, Conrad would spend days designing elaborate, creative welcomes for them: treasure hunts to find the house key, projectiles that flew out of homemade contraptions, huge painted "Welcome Home" banners. The preparation and anticipation were great fun for Conrad, and now, 45 years later, the memory of those homecomings and the antics that ensued still makes his son smile.

Owning your role in the process

It quickly became clear to us while conducting these interviews that we can make conscious behavioral choices that improve the aging trajectory and ease the burden on our loved ones as we age. It's actually quite liberating to think that we have more control over both our own mental outlook and the pace at which we age than we once thought.

And, like our interviewees, we can be inspired by role models to take similar action in our own lives. Instead of complaining, we can choose to focus on the good things. Rather than instilling guilt, we can create an atmosphere around us that makes people want to stay and visit. We can be kind instead of critical, gracious instead of grasping, and open-minded instead of judgmental. We can be proactive instead of passive, accepting responsibility for our own fate rather than forcing our children to be decision-makers in times of high stress. All of this will make us people others want to be with—and this is, actually, a matter of personal choice.

As a number of our interviewees said, each of us wants to become a person others want to be around. People choose how they wish to spend their time; if we want people to want to spend time with us, we have to be someone they will choose to be with. When we choose to live our lives with agency, we are far more likely to attract the kind of life we want—and the kinds of people we want in our lives—as we enter and live our later years.

CHAPTER TWO
GROWTH

....

How We Stay Adaptable and Manage Change

Change is hard for almost everyone. We are wired to continue to do that which comes most easily to us, or that to which we have become accustomed. Yet from our interviews we learned that in large part it is the ability to change and grow that truly distinguishes those who enjoy later life from those who fear it. As it turns out, people are far more likely to feel fulfilled, engaged, and purposeful in old age if they believe they are not yet finished growing and learning—and if they act on that belief by being open and adaptable.

We tend to think of older people as being set in their ways: you can't teach an old dog new tricks. Researchers in a University of Hamburg study wrote, "In older adults there is a clear societal expectation that they will become passive and inactive."[14] Yet there is no scientific reason to believe this must be so. Over the past half century, many studies[15] have shown that, contrary to what society leads us to believe, people are actually able to develop the creative sides of their brains more easily when they are older, not less. The Hamburg researchers found that three key elements were necessary to cultivate a creative mindset: openness to new situations, the ability to accommodate new knowledge (and to work at it), and the willingness to return to non-expert status and work with others.

How do we foster these characteristics in later life? Stanford University psychologist and researcher Carol Dweck has spent decades trying to understand what makes some people strive and thrive—living fulfilling lives—while others of equal ability or intellect fail to thrive. In her book *Mindset: The New Psychology of Success*, she argues that it comes down to whether we have a fixed mindset or a growth mindset.[16] The fixed mindset is preoccupied with other people's judgments, whereas the growth mindset is intent on continual improvement of the self. The good news is that the optimal mindset for living fully and feeling satisfied—the growth mindset—can be cultivated.

As we will see, change, growth, and creativity are inextricably entwined. Our interviewees confirmed that harnessing a growth mindset to manage and perhaps even capitalize on change is key to aging well.

Propelled by a learner's mind

Life is full of transitions—those we choose and those that are foisted upon us—that require us to step into the unknown. "This constant uncertainty may make everything seem bleak and almost hopeless," writes Sogyal Rinpoche, author of *The Tibetan Book of Living and Dying*, "but if you look more deeply at it, you will see that its very nature creates gaps, spaces in which profound chances and opportunities for transformation are continuously flowering—that is, they can be seen and seized."[17]

One of the most difficult aspects of managing change is when we do not know where we are headed and what we are working toward. Aging, in many ways, is the ultimate unknown. After all, we cannot know what is in store for us as we age: Will we live five, 10, or 20 more years? Will our loved ones outlive us? Will we remain healthy? Will our minds stay sharp?

How did our interviewees manage this uncertainty? As you will see, by staying curious rather than fearful, and by focusing on the new skills they could master rather than the unknowns they could not.

Our interviewee Raymond dedicated much of his career to managing the financial firm that he and his partners founded north of Boston. He loved everything about his work—from managing his employees to discovering new industries—and the business consumed most of his time. As a child he had many hobbies, including drawing and music, but his aptitude for finance propelled him to business school, and other interests took a back seat as he focused his energies largely on his career and family.

But always a forward thinker, Raymond looked around in his 50s and realized that a day would come when he would retire—and that when that day came, the work and people that currently filled his days would go away. The inevitability of this reality primed his curiosity, opening his mind to exploring interests he could cultivate so he would be better prepared to pursue them down the road. He and his wife, Stacy, had bought a vacation home in Arizona when their children were young, and Raymond had found over the years there that he was intrigued by the sport of cattle roping. Originally developed by cowboys whose daily work required them to quickly catch and restrain calves, roping is now a recognized rodeo sport, where top riders can lasso a calf, dismount from their horse, and tie a restraint around the calf in seven seconds. Raymond, drawn to the speed and agility of the horses and the precision of the riders in controlling the horse and casting the rope, decided this looked like something he would like to learn how to do.

Recognizing that he is a one-on-one learner, Raymond decided to hire a mentor—a local roper who could come to his ranch and teach him how to do it. He explained his approach this way: "Having resources allows you to do things... How many years do I have? I don't have the time to learn this on my own. I need a crash course. Someone has to get me going and feed me with a fire hose." Over the next decade, as he wound down his involvement in the day-to-day management of the business, Raymond invested the time he freed up into learning the art of roping and eventually competing, often against much younger riders.

Raymond laughed ruefully as he explained that it certainly wasn't always easy, and that he had to be willing to make a fool of himself from time to time. Roping requires physical stamina and the ability to control a horse with a light touch of the reins. There is precision involved in the throwing of the rope, and there are many, many ways to make a mistake. But Raymond is an initiator, someone who has confidence in his ability to learn, and he does not feel the need for perfection.

He sees no shame in trying and failing. "It's not always pleasant to be embarrassed or make mistakes, but I think you just have to do it... When you stop learning, stop evolving with what's happening out there, you drop off and become irrelevant. I didn't want to be one of those people who think they know everything."

Raymond applied this same kind of inquisitive, adventurous thinking to other areas of his life as well. For instance, when he was invited back to his high school for his 50th class reunion, he was intrigued by the idea of how to make the reunion more interesting. The idea came to him that it would be fascinating to track how his classmates' lives had changed over the years and map this evolution to the seismic societal shifts that had played out during that time. Although he knew little about filmmaking, Raymond hired a documentarian he could partner with and embarked on a project of interviewing classmates all around the country and editing these discussions into a film on the topic.

A year later, Raymond had had a crash course in filmmaking and the film he and his partner created played not only at the reunion to grateful reviews, but also at numerous film festivals around the country. "I don't know what these people know," he said of the experts he has hired. "Everyone out there knows something. You have to respect that. I can learn from them."

Raymond is not the only person to have observed this. Clayton Christensen, author of *How Will You Measure Your Life?* and a professor at Harvard Business School, has seen this principle in action in countless businesses as well as hundreds of his students over the years. "If your attitude is that only smarter people have something to teach you, your learning opportunities will be very limited," he writes. "But if you have humble eagerness to learn something from everybody, your learning opportunities will be unlimited."[18]

From the familiar to the new

Being in our comfort zones means behaving such that our activities fit routines that minimize risk and stress. In other words, we do what we are familiar with because it feels safe. There are benefits to this approach, and limitations. To lead a richer life, we actually need to operate from a space in which our stress levels are higher than usual. This is called "optimal anxiety"—it keeps us on our toes. We become more observant, are able to absorb and use new and complex information, persevere longer at challenging activities, and use our imaginations more. The key is finding the right balance and using the anxiety of going outside our comfort zones to fuel action and exploration.

One of our interviewees from the last chapter, Margo, spent 30 years living just outside New York City, teaching high school biology. She loved working with young people and watching them mature and learn. When she and her husband retired, she registered for history courses at the local community college because she decided she "needed it for her head." Life without a daily commitment to work simply was not rich enough cerebrally. All her life she had been steeped in science, and suddenly she found that learning about history opened her eyes to new ways of seeing the world. "It really grabbed me," she said, her voice full of excitement.

A few years later her husband passed away and Margo found herself lonely in her house in the suburbs. As we saw in the previous chapter, she decided to become an active agent in her life, and one way of doing this was by exploring new opportunities for growth. She began taking a variety of courses at the Teachers' Union in the city—from history, to quilting, to beading. "Sometimes I'm actually frightened when I have to do all this alone," she said about her continuing efforts to explore and engage. "Sometimes I pull back. But what else do I have to do? And I say, 'Just go, just try it, you can always leave!' I always feel that if you don't take the risk, you don't get anywhere. Sometimes it works, sometimes it doesn't, but that's life."

Margo's daughter, Hannah, feels the benefits of her mother's inquisitive nature and resilience and says she is continually learning things from her. "Mom always wants to learn new things," she explained. "She's just so curious... She keeps her brain moving."

Our interviewee George, now 72, has always been one to enjoy pushing himself a little. He sees every day as an opportunity: instead of resting on his laurels or becoming too routinized, he tries to challenge himself either physically or mentally. "I never go home the same way twice," he said, to explain his philosophy of always wanting to try something new (his children call these "Dad's long cuts"). He and his wife, Jean, take active vacations, choosing walking or biking-based tours where they are forced to interact with different cultures on the ground. In this way he and Jean have traveled around Central America and Asia. Next they will be walking the Camino de Santiago in Spain, and then heading to Portugal for a biking trip. They train physically to ensure they are fit enough to enjoy the trips, and read up on each place so they understand the culture from afar before immersing themselves in it close up.

On these trips, George learns so much both from his interactions with the people and from the immersion in different cultures that he feels simply taking photos and telling stories is not a satisfying enough way to process what he's learning. About 10 years ago, he launched a blog in which he records his travels. "Vacations are too valuable an experience not to record," he said. His goal with his posts is less about sharing his reflections with the world (although he's always happy when a grandchild reads a post!) than about finding an outlet to explore more deeply what he is learning and how it impacts his thinking.

While travel is cited by many as a way to stretch beyond the everyday and the familiar, sometimes the next adventure can be right in our own homes. Many interviewees—Judy, Jack, Henry, Gloria, Joseph, and George, to name just a few—talked about the importance of reading broadly. It keeps their minds fresh, helps them learn new things, and also gives them interesting things to talk about with others. Gloria joined a group that spent the past seven years collectively reading and discussing Proust's *Remembrance of Things Past*. George sees this time in his life as a chance to read all the literature he did not manage to read when he was younger. Last year he finished reading all of Hemingway's works, and his plan is to read all of Shakespeare's plays in time for the 400th anniversary of his death. Henry reads John F. Kennedy's and Winston Churchill's speeches and devours anything on British and American history.

At a time in life when it would be easy to simply rely on activities that have already been mastered—that are therefore familiar and easy—our interviewees were dedicated to moving beyond the familiar. "You'll be the same person five years from now except for the books you read, the places you travel, and the people you meet," said our interviewee Michael, who sees free time as nothing more than an excuse to keep learning.

Forcing ourselves to stay current

For many years, Judy, the spiffy 70-something-year-old we met earlier—worked as a college lecturer and small-business owner. When she and her husband slowed down their work schedules, she enjoyed the freedom of traveling and spending time with their grandchildren. But when it became clear to her that her lovely jewel of a local library was in danger of being shut down, she became involved in spite of herself. She had never planned on being a leader in the effort to save it or run it, yet she found herself drawn in by its serenity and beauty, its impact on the community, and the thrill of being surrounded by books and the chance to continue learning.

"Each day is an opportunity for activity and engagement," she said. "It doesn't have to be momentous, but you have to get out there and use your brain, your wits." She learned to use the library's computer program and became adept at designing and distributing evites to charity readings and events. She has paid for tutoring and even puts herself on social media to stay connected, though she generally detests it. "Staying current is a must," she explained. "It's like the Gutenberg—you're dead if you don't stay up with it."

It turns out that being comfortable with new technology is important both to staying connected and to continual learning. Our interviewee Paul told us, "If you don't [text] message, you won't hear from your grandchildren... You have to try to keep up or you'll be left out and be isolated." He even sees benefits in his struggles to understand and use this modern technology: it offers opportunities to learn from the smart young people he hires to come to his home to help him work his gadgets.

In 2013, a group of Canadian high school students taught a bunch of 80- and 90-year-olds living in a retirement community to become computer literate, in an effort to see whether—and how—it might improve their lives. The ensuing documentary, *Cyber-Seniors*, revealed that the benefits were far greater than simply connecting with family members over Skype. Shura, 88, started filming YouTube cooking tutorials; Ellard, 89, reached out to long-lost World War II friends; Barbara, 90, found ways to refresh her understanding of the world despite her difficulties with short-term memory. Others found online romance, learned to sing, and reconnected with estranged family members. Technology opened up the world for them and allowed them to do so many of the things that are critical in later life, from connecting to others to reaching beyond the confines of what they had already learned.

Being conversant in technology is also a way for older people to understand more completely the various ways younger family and friends engage with the wider world. Ian, an entrepreneur from the New York area, recently posted a picture on Facebook of his 94-year-old father holding an iPhone in one hand and the book *iPhone for Dummies* in the other. Wearing thick glasses with heavy black frames, his father squints uncertainly at the book. "But he's game to try," said Ian. "It's not easy for him, but he knows it's the only way to keep up with us these days, and he really wants to stay in the mix and know what's going on." It is easier to stay current and feel connected to the modern world when we make the effort to keep up with the times.

Developing a capacity for growth and reinvention

In the previous chapter we met Diane, who decided to be an agent in her life by embracing adventures on her own, despite being cripplingly shy. A corollary to the growth mindset is a capacity for reinvention, an ability to shift into a new identity and become someone else entirely—to rewrite the script that defines how we think of ourselves.

After taking her first solo trip—a two-week-long museum

tour of Paris—Diane realized she was so eager to learn and grow that she was willing to put herself in situations that had previously seemed too daunting. She committed to traveling on her own once a year, focusing on tours that centered on art; her goal, she said, was to get out of her comfort zone. She started seeing possibilities where previously she had seen only limitations. With two children still needing her to be available and flexible, she had never considered putting her needs first—now she realized she could go back to school part time and juggle her studies alongside her other commitments.

She decided to apply for a graduate program in social work. At first it was tough going: as she sat in a room full of younger students, Diane had to overcome her fear of failure. Could she still learn as quickly as she had when she was a college student? She spent hours laboring over her first essay for class, handed it in, and then received a call from the teacher that very night: the essay was so disjointed she would have to rewrite it. Her heart sank.

In that moment, she had to decide whether she had the ability and the will to excel, or whether she would give up. She doubled down, determined to learn from her errors: she rewrote the essay and aced it. This is the growth mindset in action. After this episode, Diane felt that every time she took a risk, she was rewarded in some profound way. "I can't even see the link between where I was and where I am now," she said. "It just started happening. It wasn't like there was any grand scheme."

These experiences have given her newfound and empowering confidence. "It opened up my world to different avenues, and this is so important," she said. "I've changed my whole being in terms of what I put in my mind." For instance, a few years ago Diane reconnected with an old college professor of hers and bartered with him: she would help him organize his papers if he would allow her to learn from him and earn continuing-education credits. "It changed both our lives," she said. Now they are collaborating on a book together about their research.

On a recent trip to Amsterdam, Diane met a young woman in the street and they struck up a conversation. It might have ended there, but Diane has developed a curiosity about people and the world that leads her to embrace new adventures at every turn. She found the girl utterly charming, and they chatted for so long that they decided to meet the following day to explore the city together. Once underway the next day, they both kept wanting to go on to the next activity, and then the next—first a museum, then lunch, then a walking tour of the city. This was the same trip to Amsterdam in which Diane, once afraid to drive four hours on her own, boarded a city bus on her own to explore untraveled parts of the city. Reflecting on this and the other aspects of her reinvented life, Diane marvels, "If you'd told me 15 years ago that I'd be doing all these things, I would have said, 'You're out of your mind!'"

The brain keeps growing, despite age and circumstance

Scientists used to believe that the brain was capable of rejuvenating only in youth, but recent research has proven that it remains plastic far longer than we previously understood. Neuroplasticity is the brain's ability to reorganize itself by forming new neural connections—and it turns out this can actually happen throughout life, in response to changing environments or trauma. When we learn a new skill through focus and practice, the sharper we become: new neural pathways are forming in response to our learning efforts. Equally, our brain undergoes "synaptic pruning"—elimination of the pathways we no longer need—when we cease to use it actively. This phenomenon of brain plasticity means that neurons in the brain are able to compensate for change, deterioration, or injury, and adjust their activity in response to new situations or changes in their environment.

And this change can happen at any age. When Donald's 85-year-old mother, Katherine, moved to an assisted-living community, the dramatic change in her demeanor and outlook proved to him that neuroplasticity was possible far into old age. "She was the poster child for that," he said.

Katherine had been living in a condo in Florida for almost two decades, since just before the death of her husband. "All the people she was spending time with in this apartment complex were angry, depressive, and sick," her son said. They did nothing much beyond playing cards and complaining. His mother was not engaged in life and had stopped making an effort with her activities or her appearance. She had no system for taking her medications and as a result was taking far too many of some and too few of others. She never went to the doctor and had no one looking after her. She had clearly lost her zest for life.

It became clear that something had to change. Donald and his wife flew down from Illinois to impress upon her that things could be different and better. For her own benefit, it was time for her to move closer to them in Chicago. Grimly, she agreed, but only because she felt she had no other choice. She had never wanted to be relegated to an assisted-living situation, seeing it as a type of death sentence.

But after just a few weeks of moving into the high-end care

facility, Katherine seemed like an entirely new person. "She decided she wanted to restart her life," Donald said. "It was incredible!" Taking a look around her new apartment, she timidly asked if she might buy new things—even though she had shown no interest in getting anything new after her husband's death. In one day flat, mother and son outfitted the entire apartment. She began breaking free of old patterns and rediscovering her interest in life and in other people. For years she had been stuck playing bridge in a group she did not like because one member constantly cheated. After the move, "she announced that she was never going to play cards again. She wanted change," Donald said, laughing. The administration and her son attended to all of her medical issues, such as getting her a hearing aid and new glasses, and established a new routine for her that was healthy and invigorating.

At this point Katherine was already in her mid-80s, yet she was making countless new friends and starting activities she would never have dared try before. "She went from having the most negative attitude to having the most positive attitude ever," her son said. "She fell in love with the people [in the community], and they fell in love with her. After six months, she was going to 10 gym classes a week." She attended concerts and lectures and spent Sundays with her family. When trying new activities, at first she would be hesitant, but as soon as she got positive feedback, she felt encouraged to do more. All her life, for instance, she had been afraid of swimming, but the fitness coordinator suggested she try swimming with water wings; after that they couldn't get her out of the pool. She gained 18 pounds from eating well, and her attitude changed from "woe is me" to "lots of people have it worse." Moving into assisted living meant that "she was freed up to have a ball," said Donald.

Three years later, when Katherine passed away at age 88, 250 people came to her funeral and she was described in the eulogies as the most positive and generous person they knew. "At the end," her son explained, "she said, 'I've had a great life, and I wouldn't have traded the last three years for anything.'"

An opportunity to keep growing

When George was still based in the Detroit area, working in engineering, he noticed that his mother was becoming more forgetful and isolated. He became increasingly worried about her safety. She was essentially housebound and dependent on her family for all human interaction. At age 95 she suffered a crisis and fell into a coma; they thought she wouldn't make it from the hospital back home. But when George moved her into a nursing facility, everything changed. "It was like a resurrection. She went from nearly dead to being the life of the party," George said. "It was like she said, 'Cancel the funeral!'"

Learning to adapt—and to continue growing—is important not only for improving the quality and enjoyment of life but also for staving off declines in cognitive ability. Lifelong learning develops something called our "cognitive reserve," which acts as a buffer against decline in brain function. This kind of cognitive decline happens when nerve connections are blocked and the signal from one nerve cannot get across the synaptic divide to reach another nerve. When we have a deeper cognitive reserve, we have more potential pathways and the blocked signal re-routes itself to a pathway that it can still use.

Sally Rosenfield, Senior Vice President of the Cure Alzheimer's Fund, explained it to us this way: our brains want to be on the back burner, doing routinized activities because it is far easier for us. But the challenge is to push ourselves to put our brains on the front burner instead.

People build cognitive reserve best by learning something completely new, rather than through mental acuity games, which can quickly become routine. Research shows the value of taking on the taxing mental challenge of learning an entirely new skill—such as a new language or a new sport—as many of our interviewees have done. A compendium of new studies under the aegis of the Stanford Center on Longevity overtly questioned the claims made by companies producing brain games, saying, "The promise of a magic bullet detracts from the best evidence to date, which is that cognitive health in old age reflects long-term effects of healthy, engaged lifestyles."[19] Over 70 psychologists, cognitive scientists, and neurologists maintained that time spent reading, socializing, gardening, exercising, or engaging in other physical and mental activities is better for the long-term health of our brains.

So, while a change as dramatic as moving into an assisted-living community might seem daunting, the benefits of what people might learn through the process—about themselves, others, or new activities that are opened up to them—offer significant physical, cognitive, and emotional advantages. Talking about his mother, George said, "She's thriving for the first time. She's in charge at the nursing home, doing things she never did. Before, her life revolved around her nieces and her small house. It was a very confined, narrow life." Whereas previously George's mother was unable to go anywhere on her own, now she plays bingo, gets her hair done every week, and has become a clotheshorse. He is seeing her life change and brighten up. "She has a very good

outlook," he said. "[I]t is so much better than when she was staying at home, watching *COPS* and sleeping most of the day and
then staying up all night."

Care facilities or group homes are, of course, not necessarily
the answer for everyone, but being in an environment where the
elderly can be active and at least somewhat independent from
their families seems to be critical to opening up unexpected possibilities for later-life contentment.

Shifts in perspective

In the face of vulnerability or loss of ability, it is equally important to keep a growth mindset. Gloria has lived in Arlington,
Massachusetts for almost her entire life. At 88 years old, she continues to be highly active and engaged in the world around her. A
renowned painter and designer, she had an illustrious career and
three children.

When Gloria's husband died 16 years ago, she found herself
bereft. He had been a musician, and day and night their house
had been filled with music—whether he was playing the piano or
the flute or listening to a recording of a Beethoven or Bach sym-
phony. After he was gone, the house seemed eerily quiet and left
her feeling disconsolate. She decided to study music composition;
it felt connected in a core, mathematical way to her work in the
design field, and she loved the sense of immersion.

Then, after 12 years of studying, her hearing began to deteriorate and she had to give it up. "I let go of it," she said. "Being
able to be adaptable is very important—to assess the situation…
Just as one acquires [abilities] at different ages, so one leaves them
behind." Gloria has once again shifted her activities to take into

account her new reality, while still immersing herself in stimulating experiences. Although she can no longer study music, she attends concerts in her hometown and in Boston all the time. "Aging gracefully is something one learns," she explained. "The trick is being able to let go but hold onto our core selves. Maybe we had to give up something, but we add something else... 'I can't do it this way, but I'll do it that way,' or 'I can't do it at all, but I'll do this instead.'"

Another interviewee, Michael, also shared a story about benefiting from growth when he shifted his focus to a new endeavor. In his case it was in an unlikely area. As a young man growing up in Philadelphia, he spent many hours on the clay tennis court at his local country club. He played avidly throughout his teen years and young adulthood and enjoyed the social life and physical challenge of continuing to play once he and his wife moved south to Florida. As he reached his 60s, however, the game began to bore him; it was simply no longer challenging enough. A friend suggested yoga, and he thought he would give it a try. "One of the challenges for high-profile, CEO-type people, used to accolades and success, is when you take up something new—golf, yoga— it's much more difficult to stay the course," he said, "not because the sport is hard but because the humiliation in front of other people is hard. You're bad, you're embarrassingly bad!"

Michael was always the oldest student in the class, and the second session was so grueling that he had to crawl out of the classroom on his hands and knees, he told us while chuckling. "You have to just persevere through this and say you'll stick with it," he said. Like Raymond, who was not afraid to make a fool of himself while learning to rope calves, Michael suffered the indignities of his yoga struggles with equanimity and good humor.

Just as Donald's and George's mothers had done, Michael and Gloria discovered that even in later life they could master new patterns, with will and some effort. When people recognize within themselves the capacity to change and learn, when they embrace a growth mindset, their lives only get richer. "It's like transposing a [musical] theme or variations on a theme," Gloria said. "[Aging] takes a theme and brings it into a new form."

Or, as Albert Einstein said, "Once we accept our limits, we go beyond them."

When change is good

How can we harness our creative minds to manage, and perhaps even capitalize on change? How can we learn to have a growth mindset? The first step is to accept that change is underway and will continue to occur; the second is to focus more on what the process of change allows us to gain than on what it forces us to lose. This requires a willingness to adapt. In his book *Aging as a Spiritual Practice*, Lewis Richmond defines adaptability as embracing potential: "Everything changes… this is the first lesson of Buddhism and the first lesson of aging," he writes. "[T]he process of transformation—aging and its accomplishments—can be very positive, with new possibilities, fresh beginnings, a wealth of appreciation, and a depth of gratitude that profoundly affects how our lives proceed."[20]

Creating the kinds of learning and growth opportunities we have explored in this chapter is an excellent use of financial resources in later life. If we see ourselves as a continuing development project we are willing to invest in, we can continue to grow indefinitely. Like Raymond, we can hire mentors to teach us new skills; like Margo, we can reach beyond the familiar to embrace the new; or like Gloria, we can commit to diving deeply into activities we have always been intrigued by but never had much time to investigate. We may produce lasting creative products such as a book of our writings or photographs. We may travel to new places for immersion in an unfamiliar culture. Or we may just open our minds to a creative, inquisitive outlook on life that allows us to learn new things and see things differently, right where we are.

As we have seen here, the unavoidable changes that come with aging can bring unexpected freshness to lives that may otherwise become stagnant. "The capacity to take a fresh look at things makes a young person out of an old person," writes Dr. George Vaillant, Professor at Harvard Medical School and former Director of the Harvard Study of Adult Development. "Play, create, learn new things and, most especially, make new friends. Do that and getting out of bed in the morning will seem a joy."[21] In countless stories, we see people who have been flexible enough to embrace change and, by being willing to grow and learn, have enriched their later years immeasurably.

CHAPTER THREE
ENGAGEMENT

....

The Energy in Finding Connections to Others

In 1938, a seminal study of aging called the Harvard Study of Adult Development was launched. Its goal was to learn about the conditions that promote optimal health and potential, and it followed the lives of 724 men, comprised of undergraduates from Harvard and a group from Boston's poor neighborhoods. Over the years participants were asked, in a variety of different ways, "What makes you happy?" After 75 years, 60 of those original participants are still alive and the study has grown to include 2,000 of the original participants' children. It is the longest study ever conducted on what makes us age well.

And the study's overarching conclusion? The participants who lived the longest and reported being the happiest were those who remained engaged with others throughout life and into old age, whether romantically or through friendships, work, and community. "Good relationships keep us happier and healthier, period," says Robert Waldinger, current Director of the study, in his TED talk. "The people in our 75-year study who were the happiest in retirement were the people who actively worked to replace workmates with playmates."[22]

In Western societies, the well-off older generation tends to have a bucket-list approach to later life, in which exciting goals are set and met, one by one. The focus is often on adventure and comfort over relationships. But this can come at a price. "Rather than feeling exhilarated by a life of bucket-list adventures, they [older people] often end up feeling depressed and disconnected," writes psychiatrist Marc E. Agronin in *The Wall Street Journal*. "As they travel the world to soak up experiences, too many seniors inevitably lose track of what really matters—their connections to family, friends and community. They feel like strangers in their own homes."[23] Their peripatetic lifestyle can also deprive them of the pleasure of filling a mentor role, which had been so satisfying earlier in life.

Studies have also shown that social engagement enhances healthy aging by lowering our blood pressure and decreasing the number of stress hormones in our bodies, while encouraging more happiness hormones like dopamine, serotonin, oxytocin, and endorphin. In other words, engaging with others can extend our lives.

But if engagement is so critical to our well-being as we age, how do we make it a priority? Is it easy? Is it just for extroverts? No. Our stories are full of people challenging themselves to reach out and purposefully cultivate relationships with others.

The concept of elderhood

In traditional societies, people gained status as they aged: elders were keepers of wisdom and passed down stories, and remained an integral part of the community. In her book *The Gift of Years*, Joan Chittister explains that older people "have the authority of experience, the authority of survival, the authority of persistence. And finally, the responsibility to give the authority of example."[24] Erik Erikson, the developmental psychologist, described this stage of life as the eighth stage, which he called "integrity." "[It is] the time when we have come to the point of being able to understand our place in the world and the life we have lived in it,"[25] he writes in his book *Childhood and Society*. When people reach this point in their lives, it becomes both an honor and a responsibility to share their hard-earned experiences with others.

Work and parenthood can offer the fulfilling experience of mentoring younger people, but when our structured work lives change or our children grow up, how do we continue to benefit from this kind of dynamic exchange? These days, many people no longer think in the binary terms of "regular work life" versus "retirement;" later life increasingly offers the freedom to contribute in new and different ways.

In a project called the New Face of Work Study run by the Encore group, researchers analyzing healthy later-life habits noted, "Running throughout these findings is a vision of the post-midlife years that is inimical to the notion of decline, whether that be the precipitous cliff of complete disengagement or the more prevalent notion these days of pulling back gradually but steadily, or phasing out."[26] We saw this play out in many of our interviews, where people made conscious efforts to find ways to share what they had learned throughout their lives with others. They were not fading away or pulling out but choosing to engage.

Donald's career has shifted from academia to business and back again. Sitting in his office at one of the world's leading business schools, he gazed out the window as he thought about the process of aging. "This is the first job where I've ever felt old," he said, "and it feels great! Students really value my opinion." Throughout the day, young people rap on his door and poke their heads into his office to ask for a quick piece of advice. He takes on individual students just because he finds the interactions fun. At this stage in the game, he feels more driven by the sense of connection he gets from sharing and advising than by the satisfaction he used to feel, at the height of his career, from being a decisive leader and taking risks.

In 2007, the entrepreneur Richard Branson and the musician Peter Gabriel conceived of "The Elders," a group of people who would share their considerable experiences in a variety of fields in order to improve the world. Together with Nelson Mandela, they established a "global village" of these older people who are charged with tackling today's most pressing problems by using their collective wisdom. "They do not have careers to build, elections to win, constituencies to please," Mandela explained in a 2007 speech that launched the effort. "They can talk to anyone they please and are free to follow paths they deem right, even if hugely unpopular."[27] In the same way, as our interviewees transitioned from the responsibilities of middle age to the freedoms of their later years, they found that there was great satisfaction in harnessing their hard-earned wisdom to help others. Not only could they make a difference in other people's lives, they themselves could benefit too.

Sharing our experiences

Lawrence, who founded a boutique investment-banking firm

in San Francisco, believes that the most important aspect of life revolves around the work we do helping others. "A life well-lived is about helping others, about building and maintaining excellent relationships with family, friends, and colleagues," he said. "The best 'monument' is the impression one leaves in the lives of those upon whom [we] had a very positive impact." This is a guiding principal in how he lives his life now that he is winding down from his position as founder of the firm he started almost four decades ago.

When asked what he envisions happening at the end of life, he contemplated the question for a moment. Still in his 60s, he does not yet consider himself retired or "old." Like many of our interviewees who feel young and vibrant, he has not yet thought in great detail about possible end-of-life choices; but he has thought about his funeral. Ideally, he imagines that if someone were to ask at his memorial, "Who here has Lawrence helped in some way?" the entire crowd would stand up. "My greatest joy, long-term, is being able to share what I've learned with others and apply what I've learned in the service of others," he said. He recounts that he was somewhat self-centered in his younger years, so the fact that he gets so much satisfaction from mentoring came as a surprise to him. Indeed, it has given him such a sense of reward that he continues to ramp up his mentoring commitments.

Currently, he is a confidential advisor to six or seven people who are facing difficult transitions in life or work. These are not quite close friendships and not quite work relationships, either. Lawrence engages them in hours of one-on-one discussion. This "work" is unpaid. "The payback for me is that they literally have nowhere else to turn, and they keep telling me that each conversation they have with me is helping them move toward a solution," he said. "It's very affirming that I've learned something and that I can share that with others and that helps them help themselves."

Of course, it is not always easy. While it is affirming on one hand, it is also intimidating on the other, because he is taking on an awesome responsibility. He often thinks to himself, "I better not screw this up…" While he loves his current work, when he looks to the future and imagines having fewer responsibilities at the office, he knows he will be able to parlay his skills and interests into ways to continue connecting meaningfully with others. "I love the complex problem-solving challenges. I love seeing how the elegant solutions we deliver improve the quality of people's lives," he said. "These [mentorship] activities require application of the same problem-solving skills I use in my day job."

As we saw in an earlier chapter, it was his father, Conrad, who planted the seeds of this desire to live a life of generosity and service. As head of a school in rural Colorado, Conrad ruled with a stern hand while being loved and respected by all. Lawrence admired the way his father aged, living to be 94—fully engaged with activities and people right up until he took his last breath. "He spent the last day of his life supervising teenagers who were doing chores around a piece of property he loved," Lawrence said. "He spent the afternoon working in his silver shop. He was a highly skilled silversmith, and that was his hobby. He had dinner with my brother and his family. After dinner he sat down on the couch and quietly passed away."

Lawrence's father continued to have a special connection to young people well past the age of his retirement. "Even today, people with whom I grew up talk about how my father was one of the biggest influences in their lives." This example of mentorship has been powerful in Lawrence's life and guides him toward prioritizing activities as he ages that allow him to continue to be an active, positive influence in the lives of others.

Improving the health of our brains

We saw in our chapter on growth that the brain remains plastic—capable of change and growth—for longer than most people realize. According to a study conducted by researchers in Chicago, there is evidence that socializing may actually improve our brain function. Researchers at the Rush Memory and Aging Project followed over 1,000 people, with an average age of around 80, for five years. None of the participants had dementia at the start of the study. They found that the most socially active seniors experienced a 70% reduction in the rate of cognitive decline, compared with their less social peer group. Since the study was following people over a period of time, and started when they were mentally healthy, the authors argue that the findings suggest that it was the lack of sociability that caused a greater risk of mental decline, rather than the other way around.

"Socializing relieves stress, and there's a huge connection between stress and problems with the brain as we get older," says Bryan James, an epidemiologist and lead researcher. "Lack of social contact is stressful for all social animals, and high chronic stress increases risk of cardiovascular disease, some cancers, obesity, all mental illnesses and addictions."[28]

More fascinating still is that researchers believe the benefits can be even greater if the social interaction brings us into contact with someone who is different from us in age, socioeconomic background, or interests. They say that the experience of diversity enhances creativity by encouraging the search for new information and fresh perspectives, which in turn leads to better decision-making and problem-solving. "Diversity jolts us into cognitive action in ways that homogeneity simply does not," writes Katherine W. Phillips in *Scientific American*, which analyzed a series of studies by organizational scientists, psychologists, sociologists, economists, and demographers. "When disagreement comes from a socially different person, we are prompted to work harder."[29] This is because we are forced to communicate more fully to bridge the gap, instead of relying on mental shortcuts.

In the previous chapter, we met Judy, a former professor from Connecticut who became an initially reluctant leader in the effort to save her town's library. Being involved in activities at the library brings her into contact with the young and old, the wealthy and struggling, intellectuals and consumers of pop culture, and she has grown to appreciate interacting with people of various ages and backgrounds. "When you get to be towards 70, if all your friends are near 70, that's a pretty tight silo to be in, and that's not healthy," she said. "It's important to interact with others who are different from you because otherwise you get set in your ways and you're in a rut."

She now gets huge satisfaction out of connecting with people outside her immediate social circle, whether through mentorship opportunities or volunteering. Through this, she's "become more aware of the importance of critical relationships; being not just the beneficiary but also the giver."

Judy joins groups to be engaged with others, "to bring out others and let them bring me out," she said. "We bolster ourselves, and support each other." She is constantly discovering different ways to connect; everywhere she has traveled, for example, she finds that people who play tennis are people she enjoys being around. Equally, she enjoys conversing with readers, and for the past 13 years has been part of a reading group that meets every month. The participants are all different ages and backgrounds, and come from a range of towns in the area of Connecticut where she lives.

She credits the diversity of the interactions in the group with making her life richer. She explains, "When the physical self can't sustain, you have to do a lot of your living through imagining things." This is easier to do when our circles are larger and our friends more varied.

And also, sometimes hanging out with younger people is simply fun. Our interviewee Jean, who now lives in a spacious lake house in Virginia, opens her home not only to friends and family but also to friends of her children and grandchildren. She loves to have the house full of people of all ages, running around and enjoying themselves. Hosting them seems no chore at all: "I like being with them. It's exciting to see what they're up to," she said. "It keeps you younger!"

It takes some courage to branch out and interact with others whose lifestyle and experiences might be different from our own, but our interviewees believe the efforts pay off. Many also made the point that if a connection or relationship does not take root or prove enjoyable, it's hardly the end of the world. Helen, the lively real estate entrepreneur we met in Chapter One, told us, "If it [a new friendship] doesn't work out, I'll move on. You can't be broken up about the time that you spent."

Branching out beyond family

As we talked with people about their later lives, we noticed an interesting pattern emerge in their stories of engagement: many of our interviewees were focused on developing relationships beyond family, rather than depending on family relationships. Even though their families remained closest in their hearts, it turns out many of our interviewees did not actually spend the majority of their time with family members—in fact, just the opposite.

Surprisingly, it seems that this can actually be better for us in the long run. Journalist Barbara Bradley Hagerty was skeptical of this assertion and set about reviewing multiple recent studies published in medical journals both in the U.S. and abroad, only to discover that they all pointed to the same conclusion: having robust friendships is healthier for us, mentally and physically, than close family relationships. "Friends are kind of the Swiss Army knife of relationships. They do everything, boosting your health, lengthening your life, preserving your memory, helping your career, gentling the aging process," she writes in her book *Life Reimagined*. "[F]riends bestow a purer, less complicated emotional and biological reward than family does."[30]

When our interviewee Helen moved to Florida some years ago, she made a conscious decision to build new relationships rather than relying on her large extended family—four children, three stepchildren, and 15 grandchildren—for her social life. She had always valued having diverse relationships. Decades ago, as a single divorcee, she worked full time in real estate, managing 150 brokers in five offices around the country. When she remarried 30 years ago, she continued her work and many activities; she loved the opportunity work gave her to interact with different people. But when her husband wanted to uproot them and move south,

Helen needed to reassess her situation. Though a number of her children lived just a short drive away, she had no friends in Florida, and no professional ties.

But she has used her gift with people to make inroads, and has built herself a robust community. "You have to keep and hold onto relationships and constantly reach out to the community," she explained. She appreciates connections she has made with a creative group of theater people and local artists. Each week she is out to dinner with one of these friends, and once a year she travels with a group of them to exotic places. "You need to open yourself up to others to get a response," she said. "To sit and do nothing is the worst, and the easiest thing to do. You have to get out of your chair, go out. Stop futzing!"

"Family is different. It's not fair to rely on family. They've got their own things going on," she said. "I never leaned on my kids very much." The people she now interacts with in her daily life give her enormous pleasure and keep her occupied. Currently, she is on the Board of an Ivy League school, sits on her city council, is a member of the architectural review committee, serves as the development chair for a golf club, and is deeply involved in experimental local theater. She loves to collect art and has become a docent at a large new art museum. "My outlook is tied to what I'm doing in my life. There are all kinds of different people and different exposures in my life," she said. Despite her large family, she thrives off the many relationships she has built outside of that structure. And when she does get together with family, she finds she is less demanding of them and feels more genuinely engaged in what is happening in their lives.

Karen—our interviewee with the Spanish mother—also went through a move that she thought would be challenging, and, though it was easier than expected, it changed the way she related to others. At age 67, she and her husband, Will, moved from their tight-knit neighborhood in suburban Philadelphia to a large, wooded community in North Carolina, where they knew only two couples. They had moved around earlier in their lives, but that had proven to be relatively easy because of their two children; being young parents had given them a natural entry point into conversations and activities. Now she had to come up with reasons to connect with new people by herself. "It takes a concerted effort when you move," she said. "You have to take the initiative yourself, whatever your interest level is."

Their new apartment complex included a number of buildings clustered around a pool and activity center. One of the buildings was said to have a very active population, and Karen made a point of choosing that one. On a warm spring morning, the movers arrived with their furniture, and they settled into an apartment on the tenth floor. Because she and Will don't play golf or tennis, she had been worried about how they would meet people of different ages. But it turns out there were so many social events that they had no problem meeting a variety of new people. Over time, she got in the habit of throwing casual dinner parties, and two or three times a month she hosts friends in their dining room. And the building staff even makes socializing easy: if anyone needs an extra table or more chairs, they just have to ask.

"You have to stay engaged in your own way," Karen said. "You don't want your family to be your whole life. Your kids have their own lives, you can't depend on them for your happiness. I would be a lonely person if I was just waiting on my kids to take care of me!"

Finding ways to connect

We discovered through our discussions that being strategic about reaching out can sometimes mean adopting a fol-
low-the-breadcrumbs type of approach. Jack, who had been a
serial entrepreneur in the New York area, regaled us with stories
of serendipity in which he would meet someone accidentally or
connect with someone for one purpose, and then find that that
relationship would lead to something entirely different and un-
planned. Being open to chance and seizing opportunities was key.

When Jack was in his 40s, he headed out to the airport for a
flight to Boston, only to realize as he arrived that he had forgotten
his wallet in the cab. At the time, there were ads on television and
billboards for one of his businesses that featured his image, and a
stranger who recognized him from this branding approached him
as he stood in the departure lounge, frantically patting his pockets
in search of his money. They started chatting and discovered they
shared a good-natured sense of humor and a passion for baseball.
Soon they were laughing about Jack's misfortune, and the man—
Tom—ended up lending him $300 so he could catch his flight.

Jack was impressed with Tom's generosity and called him the
next day to thank him. It had occurred to him that his new friend
would be perfect for a job opening he'd been trying to fill. One
interview later, Tom had secured a new job and Jack had a new
colleague he genuinely admired. Tom became a cherished man-
ager... and some years later, he married Jack's sister. Talk about
being open to opportunities!

Being genuinely interested in people helps. Now an avid art
collector, Jack explained that his interest doesn't necessarily start
with the artwork itself, but rather because he meets and likes the
artists. He told a story about meeting one mid-century artist years

ago at a cocktail party. Jack was so impressed by the man's fascinating life story and the passion with which he talked about his creative process that he looked him up that night after returning home. Soon Jack started collecting his work, and from there branched out to meeting and collecting the art of other artists this man knew. Now, when he looks around his apartment, Jack is surrounded not just by fascinating works of art, but also by the life histories and personalities of the artists involved, many of whom he has met and gotten to know.

Oftentimes relationships come in the form of groups or organizations that our interviewees started or joined that meet regularly and enjoy an established sense of community. As a young child and teenager, our interviewee Walter had always loved playing the piano, but when he was in the thick of work and family life he could play only occasionally for himself on weekends. When he turned 50, he decided to start taking piano lessons again. Two decades later, he is a member of two local groups of amateur musicians, who play for each other in informal concerts every couple of weeks. He finds it an exhilarating experience. Sometimes his group plays in nursing homes and retirement communities, which gives him the added joy of bringing happiness to others. Connecting with people who share his love of music has been a source of great happiness for him.

After Gloria's husband died 16 years ago, when she was in her early 70s, she decided to join one of Massachusetts' oldest libraries, founded in 1807. The library is membership based, with over 200 supporters who run 15 groups with varying literary and historical interests. She drives into the city at least once a week to attend discussion groups led by scholars of, for example, James Joyce and Shakespeare; historians who give lectures on the World

Wars; and movie experts. "It's my second home," she said. She loves the mixture of gender and age she encounters there, enjoying "the excitement of sharing life with people; focusing on the same great work of literature, same concert series, and so on."

For many of our interviewees, attending a religious institution allowed them to integrate into their local communities and find a bond with people of different ages and interests. Our interviewee Paul is a Mennonite who grew up in the Midwest and has spent his career at top research institutions. He and his wife have helped microfinance small businesses as a way of supporting relief organizations connected with his church. "Those experiences are extremely rewarding," he said. "We've given to places doing good in the world; each has given us a chance to expand [our] friendships."

But where Paul has found the greatest satisfaction in the past 15 years may be in his position as an overseer of his city's orchestra. In this capacity and because of his resources, he has had the chance to develop relationships that have ended up becoming very important to him. He has been on the orchestra's annual funds committee as both a donor and fundraiser, and as a result he has come to know the conductor of the orchestra and the musicians quite well.

"It's buying friendships in one way, but they are treasured friendships," he explained. He recognizes that there is an entire world of people at the orchestra whom he and his wife would never have had the opportunity to become friends with if they had not been as generous in giving money.

Getting over the hump

We were also interested in hearing stories from our interviewees who had embarked on forming connections even when it wasn't easy for them. How did they take the leap if they were mourning the loss of a spouse, or missing a community they had known for years?

Joyce grew up the youngest of four sisters, a quiet girl who loved to read mysteries. Later, when she and her husband entered their 60s, he wanted to move from the town in Connecticut where they had lived for the last three decades into New York City. "I lost my whole community and it was very difficult for me," Joyce said. "I get a lot of enjoyment from my friends."

In Connecticut, Joyce had volunteered at a number of organizations and, through these, had formed lots of connections and close friendships. It took some time to adjust to moving and leaving these behind. She got into a funk and spent almost a year feeling sorry for herself, until one day she thought, "Oh my God, I have to stop complaining!"

"I pushed myself, but you have to be ready for it personally," she explained. "I don't like change—that's difficult for me. But then I'd think, what's the worst that can happen? I just couldn't be that person who was a complainer." She focused on what she valued (education) and where she felt familiar and comfortable (with children) and began by volunteering to teach remedial English in a local high school. There she met some people with whom she began attending a gym. After that, she took up playing Mahjong. It took four years for her to rebuild her community, but now she is content to be in the city, with so many opportunities to engage with others.

Some of our interviewees had to overcome the hurdle of

losing a spouse, and find the energy and courage to leave the house and forge new lives for themselves. They had to reinvent both how they spent time with people and who they chose to be with. When Margo's husband passed away, she had to conquer her fear of branching out into the social world afresh, this time alone. Questions would swirl in her mind before leaving the house for an activity: "Do I really want to go? What am I going to find there? Will I be accepted? Will they ignore me?" But she disciplined herself to commit to at least one activity a day. After all, she reasoned, the alternative was being stuck in the house, alone. "I have a great desire to get out and be social," she said. "What am I going to do—stay home and cry? Don't think I don't miss him, because I do. It's very lonely. But I don't want to sit around the house."

She also knows now that it is important to have a sense of perspective and not to expect everything to be perfect. "Life is not *The Brady Brunch*. Life doesn't work that way," she said. "Not everything is going to go your way. You're going to have to adjust to all sorts of situations, and you'll be happier if you learn to adjust."

The connections she has made give a sense of purpose to her days that she otherwise wouldn't have. "If I have a good conversation with someone and have a good rapport, that gives me meaning in life because you're touching someone else…emotionally and intellectually," she said. And when she volunteers to help kids who are having difficulty reading, "it's nice to be known, to be greeted." She feels as though she belongs to a caring network and is part of the fabric of a bigger life than one that revolves only around her and her needs or fears.

Her daughter finds her mother's sense of adventure and courage admirable. "I don't know if she has anxiety going into a room of people," Hannah told us, "but she doesn't let it show!"

Moving beyond judgment

Some personality types strive for perfection, and seek it in others too. For many years, Henry operated in this way: finding the one thing that was wrong as opposed to looking for all the things that were right. In business, he explained, you have to constantly sit in judgment of others, and it can be hard to be nice or encouraging. But he has used the turning points in his life—among them a divorce, a serious health scare, and a business crash—as impetus for self-reflection, finding that as he ages he has become more humble and supportive of others. "I've become more conscious of other people and my effect on other people, and it's less about me," he said. Focusing more on others than on himself has made his later-life experiences more enjoyable. "I find myself not discouraging anyone but mostly encouraging everyone," he explained. "Not in a fashion where I'm sitting in judgment...but more in a constructive way."

Sometimes it is our own preconceptions and expectations that hold us back—and yet, we found that the trope of people becoming more judgmental as they get older did not hold true with our interviewees. When we asked them whether they felt they had changed as they aged—and if so, how—the majority of them said that age had humbled them, teaching them that they did not necessarily know better than anyone else. They had, in fact, become less judgmental of others, more forgiving and open-minded. Judy put it this way: "Judging others is a bad habit; but it rubs off when you yourself start failing and can't do everything so perfectly... and you're not living up to those iron-clad expectations; that's when you become less judgmental."

Joseph, a former biologist and lifelong environmentalist, shared a story of an unlikely friendship that struck us as illustrative. For many years, a lawyer who works for a large oil company has been in Joseph's circle of acquaintances. The man, Karl, was known for his hard-ball tactics and his outsized persona. They would see each other at local events and social gatherings, and Joseph found Karl's manner off-putting. "He was bombastic, narcissistic, and a real bore," Joseph said.

Then one night they were at the same dinner party and the hostess seated them next to each other. Initially Joseph was mortified, and their conversation was stilted. But then, realizing he was stuck there for at least three courses, Joseph decided to really engage this time, to listen and to ask questions. He started to enjoy himself. The two men had an interesting discussion, covering a variety of topics from history to education, and it turned out that, one on one, the lawyer was affable and intelligent. Joseph came away pleasantly surprised, and having decided the man was worth knowing after all. They did not see eye to eye, but the evening was much more pleasant—and more interesting—than he had feared.

Some months later, the two men found themselves at an outdoor party, both headed toward the bar. Whereas previously Joseph would have assumed it was not worth the time or effort to engage with Karl, this time he decided to keep an open mind. They soon were in a robust discussion about the importance of fossil fuel and the use of oil; of course, they had wildly divergent opinions. "I didn't back off from what I knew was the truth, but I expressed it with humility and directness and a little bit of affection for him," Joseph said. They had a lively debate—at times heated but always respectful. "I know I changed his mind a little bit… It was fun."

Joseph discovered that he liked the challenge of seeing an is-sue he felt strongly about from a different perspective. He learned something useful, even if he and Karl agreed to disagree in the end, and he felt invigorated by the chance to engage in a mean-ingful dialogue that might effect change.

The two men now see each other regularly at the Sunday brunches that Joseph hosts around his pool. He feels that in becoming more patient and less judgmental, he has learned so much. "My judgment has changed," he said. "Now I consider him to be a really good friend." As he recounted this story to us, Joseph was struck by how much the relationship had changed—and by the realization that what had brought that about was not a change in Karl's personality but in how Joseph perceived it.

With maturity comes greater awareness

This tendency toward decreased judgment seemed to be part of a larger shift. A number of our interviewees talked about how their perspectives evolved from being self-focused to seeing their lives more in relation to others and becoming better listeners.

Michael, whose foray into yoga we heard about in the last chapter, had been in advertising for decades, living in Philadel-phia and running a firm that tripled in size in five years. He was driven to succeed. "When I was younger, I had something to prove," he said. "I was more self-absorbed, boastful—a braggado-cio." While this drive is in part what fueled his success, he finds that as he approaches 70, he has evolved out of that phase. He's not as interested in trying to one-up others. "I'm more interested in finding out more about the other person," he said.

Similarly, when Lawrence was younger, he remembers being brash and confident. He wanted to learn from others, but there was an arrogance to his method, and he was never big on listening. "I hope I have become kinder, a better listener, more likely to ask questions than to make assumptions, and therefore less likely to ascribe motives to the behavior of others," he said, reflecting on the ways he has changed. "Where I used to jump to conclusions based on my assumptions, I now hope I have learned to first take time to understand the other person's position."

He sees the value in fully engaging with other people's way of seeing the world. "I'm more eager to listen to others' perspectives," he said. "I remind myself that none of us do anything that we ourselves think is irrational." This allows him to put himself in others' shoes; as a result, he finds himself more focused on the greater good, on staying connected and not doing anything that would negatively impact others.

This ability to open up and finally see the people around them provided some of our interviewees with the kind of engagement that was truly life changing. Francis, now in his 80s, grew up on the Lower East Side of New York during World War II with parents who worked hard to gain a strong financial foothold for their small family. As a teenager, Francis started a business selling what were then known as trimmings: buttons, edging, sewing supplies. He married young and had three boys for whom he had high expectations, wanting them to have everything he himself had not had growing up. As a result, Francis worked twice as hard as his peers, spending long days at the office and working most weekends; he had little time for thinking outside the boundaries of his own world and personal experience.

Eventually, the pace of the work and the constraints it

imposed on his life started to wear on Francis. "For 42 years, when working, I did not reach out to help anyone else," he said. "I was very aware of what I was missing, that I wanted to go toward." Through his church, he learned of an organization that supported members of the community by going out into their homes to determine the kind of help they needed. He decided to become involved—he ended up dedicating over 15 years of his life to this effort (until several years ago when his wife's health required more of his time) and was transformed by how much the work taught him about others and about himself.

"I liked visiting people in their homes. When you begin to see the situation, you feel it more and they feel closer to you," he said. He recalled one day in particular which he remembers in detail because of how it altered his outlook. He had gone into the home of a mother seeking assistance with rent and initially felt an urge to flee the scene that confronted him there. The apartment was tiny and cluttered, and the woman lived there with her three children, one of whom was severely autistic and another who was physically handicapped and unable to manage the bathroom on his own. Overwhelmed by the magnitude of the need, Francis was at first at a complete loss. But then, trying to quell his apprehension, he focused on the reason he was there and how he could help. After an hour of sitting with the family and observing the love and care with which the mother attended to her children and their attachment to her, Francis's eyes were opened.

His prior professional life had been about being controlling and demanding, about his way being the one right way to do things. When he saw this mother, who had so little, and the fortitude and love with which she was quite resourcefully managing her situation, he realized that there "is more than one way to get there"—that the neat, corporate-world standard that had been his barometer for so long wasn't all there is, and that there is a broader world out there, with examples to see and learn from if only you look.

"I learned there are different ways to do things," he explained. "You suddenly are observing—letting yourself feel some things or see some things because you're really in the community, you're really looking… You learn things, you see the value in people… The things that you feared turned out to be better than you thought," he added, his voice thick with emotion. "When I worked at [my corporate] pace, I never looked up, but now I realize there are a lot of good people out there—bad too, but there are a lot of good ones," he said. "There are more good than bad."

His unexpected emotional connection to these people gave him a fresh perspective on the world and a defining sense of purpose. He began to pay attention to how others interacted with him and with the world around them. When his wife fell ill and had to spend two weeks in intensive care at the hospital, Francis visited her every day. He noticed that it was always the same woman who sat behind the reception desk in the main lobby, and that each day—even though a stream of people poured in and out—she made a point of greeting Francis and asking about his wife. "I'm deeply moved by people's empathy," he said, his voice cracking. Now, he says, he has been "awakened to more contact with humans," and that, "just by looking at what's going on, you find very, very caring people."

Though his wife is very ill and his days are filled with chores that he lovingly undertakes in order to help her, he is open to the beauty of everyday interactions. He spends time enjoying people and really listening to them, and he often stops to talk to others.

He can let himself feel things, see things, and really live in the moment. When we asked him for his advice on aging well, he summed up the philosophy he has come to this way: "Just allow yourself a little bit of time," he said. "Pursuing success and accumulating things—that's a small world. Make your world bigger."

Embracing a bigger world

There is no need to accept a life in which our universe shrinks as we get older. In emerging from one stage of life and entering another, our lives are immeasurably enhanced if we overcome fears, stasis, and preconceptions in order to reach out to others. We need to make sure to maintain and grow the network of people with whom we can share our experiences and from whom we can learn.

Financial resources can be a benefit here. A recent article in the *Industrial Psychiatry Journal* put it this way: "Those with more physical, material and intellectual resources also have more social 'capital,' which allows them to continue to seek out new relationships and forms of social involvement."[31] In other words, financial resources can be harnessed to cultivate a life rich with relationships and connections with others. Our interviewees shared with us a number of stories in which their assets (whether money or the time that money afforded) opened the door for them to develop friendships and connections. Yet, while the door was opened, they still had to walk through—they still had to decide to proactively take the step to reach out, nurture, and maintain these relationships.

And while resources can be helpful, they certainly aren't necessary. Book clubs, volunteering, galvanizing the neighbors—all these can be done for free. So, resources or not, don't squander the opportunity to begin branching out today. What impressed us most in the stories we heard from our interviewees was how many of these very positive relationships were new—friends they had just made, students they had just met, new employees who had just been hired and required mentoring, or new neighbors in a new town. It's never too late to begin to form the kind of lasting relationships that can provide a rich, broad, and connected perspective on the world.

CHAPTER FOUR
DRIVE

....

Maintaining a Sense of Purpose and Motivation

The conventional image of older, financially secure adults has them relaxing on the beach, hitting the ball on a verdant golf course, or lobbing a volley on the tennis court. But this idea turns out to be outdated and is actually the opposite of what we found in our discussions with our interviewees.

While the temptation is to take our foot off the gas as we age, we learned that in order to live long and happy lives, we might actually need to press down on the accelerator instead. Without motivation to engage in activities that enrich ourselves and others, giving our lives a sense of meaning, we risk becoming obsolete and spending our days focusing on negatives rather than positives. It is when we have a sense of purpose and drive that we are motivated to spring out of bed in the mornings, regardless of our numerical age.

In his book *Being Mortal*, Atul Gawande reflects on a question posed by the early 20th-century Harvard philosopher Josiah Royce: "Why does simply existing seem empty and meaningless?" Royce believed the answer was that we all seek a cause beyond ourselves. "The cause could be large (family, country, principle) or small (a building project, the care of a pet)," Gawande explains. "The important thing was that, in ascribing value to the cause and seeing it as worth making sacrifices for, we give our lives meaning." Without this sense of loyalty to some greater purpose, Royce wrote, "we have only our desires to guide us, and they are fleeting, capricious, and insatiable."[32]

There has been significant research recently into what constitutes lasting happiness and the effect it has on us, not only mentally but also physically. This current research on well-being comes from two general perspectives: one is the "hedonic" approach and defines well-being in terms of finding pleasure and avoiding pain. It is about the sensual and the internal. This kind of happiness is not so hard to find but can be short-lived and often unsatisfying in the long term. In contrast, the other approach is "eudaemonic"—a term coined centuries ago by Aristotle. It focuses on personal fulfillment, the realization of one's potential, and deriving meaning from activities. This is about having a higher purpose in life; it is not a feeling or a promise but a practice. "It's living in a way that fulfills our purpose," says Helen Morales, a classicist at the University of California, Santa Barbara, as quoted in a 2016 *New Yorker* article. "It's flourishing. Aristotle was saying, 'Stop hoping for happiness tomorrow. Happiness is being engaged in the process.'"[33] This kind of happiness is harder to achieve, but it is also more lasting and fulfilling; we are able to tap into it again and again, through a consistent drive toward meaningful experience.

One intriguing 2013 study from Carleton University and the University of Rochester asked whether experiencing purpose and drive can actually make us live longer. Researchers studied a

group of people in mid-life and determined that "having a purpose in life appears to widely buffer against mortality risk across
adult years."[34] This turns out to be partially true for purely practical reasons: in another joint study from the Universities of Michi-
gan and Wisconsin, people who claimed to have "purpose in life"
were more proactive about taking care of their health—they went
to the doctor regularly and engaged in preventative care, which
will of course enhance the overall quality of life.[35] In contrast, lack
of drive can lead to complacency, which negatively affects both
psychological and physical health.

Finding rewards that motivate

Allan was a longtime management consultant in Atlanta.
He loved working and had few hobbies other than weekly movie
nights with his wife and two boys. But once Allan entered his late
60s and started dialing down his work commitments, he began
to turn inward and examine more deeply the sources of his motivation. Yes, he wanted to find ways to have fun and relax, but
he also knew that he needed to maintain connections with others
in order to feel driven and purposeful as he aged. He recognized
that, although he is an introvert, he is high on affiliation, which
means that he really enjoys being around people. "To me, work
provides the perfect opportunity to balance that," he said.

Twice he quit his job to focus more on leisure activities and
found the days long and hard, with no sense of urgency or meaning. Twice he decided to start working again because his life felt
empty without the sense of drive he used to get from heading to
the office every day. "Part of retirement I really enjoyed, and other
parts I didn't," he explained. "I was feeling healthy and wondered,

'Do I really want to be doing this for another 30 years?' I didn't want to putter around and find things to do. You kind of feel like you're treading water and waiting to die. I've never been one who can't wait to go into the basement and start building furniture or take out the easel."

George Vaillant writes in his book *Aging Well* that there are four basic activities that make later life in retirement rewarding. The first is replacing workmates and deceased parents or friends with new friends. The second is rediscovering how to play; this not only opens us up to new friends but also "permits a person to maintain self-esteem while giving up self-importance." The third is being creative, which is an ideal pursuit in later life as it requires time and sometimes solitude, both of which become plentiful. The fourth and last is continuing to learn. "The challenge," Vaillant writes, "is to combine the fruits of maturity with the recovery of childlike wonder."[36]

As we learned in our interviews, this can happen when we tap into our deepest preoccupations and heartfelt inclinations. But how do we transcend the appeal of immediate self-gratification, find what drives us, and build toward a later life of meaning and contentment? When work, parenting, and/or running a household is our primary source of satisfaction in young adulthood and mid-life—offering us clear goals, immediate feedback, and challenges that match our abilities—how do we continue to find the same satisfaction in later life, when the rules and our desires may have changed? How do we make the kind of progress that keeps us motivated and engaged?

Discovering who we really are

Allan's conundrum nicely illustrates the two measures of

happiness we mentioned earlier: day-to-day pleasures, which are more fleeting and self-focused, and longer-term, deeper contentment, which tends to require more thought and effort to achieve. Allan discovered that in attempting to maximize the first type of pleasure during the later phase of his life, he was shying away from activities he thought would add tedium or struggle. By assuming that he valued relaxation over effort, he was removing a critical component of satisfaction from his life.

Now he is engaged in a start-up, which offers him the chance to connect with energetic young minds and mentor them in a way that feels mutually enriching. "It's nice to be able to do anything you want to do, but it's also nice doing things with other people," he said. "Helping people become better than they ever thought they could become. Thinking through strategies." This is what gives him the drive to get up and go into another office, when he had assumed that that phase of his life was over.

We met George, the former engineer originally from Detroit, when we were analyzing the benefits of agency. When he sold his company at age 51, phasing out of his intense work routine, he and his wife, Jean, moved to a gated community in central Florida where they could play golf and tennis, enjoy healthy meals at the club, and live a life of sun and leisure. After decades in the cold, with a punishing work schedule, they both believed this new lifestyle would come as a welcome relief—only to discover they were wrong.

"We were doing the retirement thing at 50 that people normally do at 65," George said. Their days consisted of golf, lunch, cocktails, naps, and then dinner with the same group of people. George and Jean had made assumptions about what they wanted, and they soon realized that they had miscalculated: they were too young for the group and bored by the activities. Their neighbors were very similar to them demographically, and though they had thought this would create a comfortable social dynamic, in fact just the opposite was true. "By the third hole [of golf] they'd ask you what you did for a living," George said. "It was a way of pegging you socially, and we came from a humble background, so that was something we just hated."

Their willingness to make the necessary changes to address their situation came both from a desire to be happy on a basic, day-to-day level and from the need to do something that felt more meaningful. As Jean explained, "It doesn't have to be set in stone that this is the phase you're in and this is the way it's got to be." George added, "We should have researched more about who we are, versus what we had."

They decided to head north, this time settling in Virginia near their daughter, who had just had a baby. There they launched into a series of rather strenuous endeavors that they never would have thought they would enjoy. First they bought and renovated a small, dilapidated lake house. Then, when their two sons and their families also moved to places nearby, they bought a much larger house that needed a huge amount of work. Rolling up their sleeves, they spent the next 12 months climbing ladders and getting on their hands and knees, doing much of the renovation themselves.

"You feel like you're sinking your teeth into something and doing something with your hands and your mind," George said. They put in plumbing, hung sheetrock, and tiled bathrooms. George was handy, and Jean was a fast learner who thrived on the challenge of the project and the joy of working together. When it came time to tile the bathrooms, she thought, why not? "I just buy books and read how to do it, and then do it," she said. "You just have to believe that you can. We are goal-driven and set goals, and then we get to the end of that goal. We communicate well. It's fun to complete goals as a team."

Our interviewee Judy shared a similar sentiment, talking about her volunteering work at the library. She quickly discovered through her work there that choosing effort over relaxation was preferable to being bored. "There are times that aren't fun, but it's worth it," she explained. "Relaxing is not something I'm good at. It's not nourishing. There's got to be more. I would rather have that tension and burden, with the other side—the pay-off of full engagement of the self." As a leader over the last six years, she has had to rise to certain occasions that she never would have had to deal with in other scenarios. "A lot of older women have found a way to be meaningful through this library," she added. "And what would all of us be doing otherwise?"

The paradox of choice

Purpose, and the drive that comes with it, is important throughout life, but it is especially important as we get older, when the immediate purpose we used to derive from work and parenting begins to wane. What should we do, if we can choose to do anything? As we age, we gain the freedom to decide what we do with our time, and that freedom can be challenging for some. Purpose becomes more self-defined than ever before.

We found an intriguing parallel here with our first book, *Raised Healthy, Wealthy & Wise*: people often suffer from a paradox of choice. How do we pick something to work toward, something that feels meaningful and has real value, when we have so many options? In the previous book, we were focusing on how purpose and drive can emerge for a young person who may not have the motivating impetus of financial necessity. We discovered that these youngsters face specific psychological hurdles, and we found through our research for this book that these hurdles may be even more challenging for older people. Older adults often have strong emotional ties to their previous driven, purposeful lives, and the sense of closing a door on a phase of life that felt rewarding can throw them off kilter.

Much of the current literature on longevity and health points to this notion of drive and purpose as being critical to older people's well-being. In her book *Life Reimagined*, journalist Barbara Bradley Hagerty interviews David Bennett, director of Rush University's Alzheimer's Disease Center, about the research he conducted into what types of mental attitude predict whether or not someone will develop dementia. The big surprise of the research was that having purpose in life was "almost a magic bullet": people with purpose are far less likely to develop dementia or experience cognitive decline, even when their autopsies reveal that they had the dementia pathology. "People with little purpose were two and a half times more likely to develop dementia than those with a mission," Bennett said.[37] And, according to his research, older people who score high on purpose in life are twice as likely to remain alive over a five-year follow-up period as those who have low scores.

In his book *Drive*, Daniel Pink explains that people are ultimately less motivated by extrinsic rewards, such as salaries or prizes, than they are by intrinsic worth. "We're learning that the profit motive, potent though it is, can be an insufficient impetus for both individuals and organizations," writes Pink. "An equally powerful source of energy, one we've often neglected or dismissed as unrealistic, is what we might call 'the purpose motive'... Humans seek novelty and challenges. They want to exercise their capacities, explore, learn."[38]

And how, practically speaking, do we recreate this sense of purpose and engagement once we have left behind the purpose-defining framework of a career and/or child-rearing?

Harnessing old skills for new purposes

In the previous chapter we shared that when Karen had to start afresh after moving to North Carolina, she found a variety of ways to begin engaging with others. But one of the most gratifying ways she moved forward was by building on skills she already had, and putting them to new uses. Back home in Philadelphia, Karen and her husband had co-run their business together for many years. She'd always been a proactive leader and a terrific organizer. This was more than work for her—it was truly a passion. She felt a strong connection to the many employees who had worked for them for decades, and she enjoyed looking after them. While working there, Karen initiated a healthy living plan as well as a drive to get team members to invest more money into the company's 401(k) plan. As a result of these efforts, the company saw a 54% increase in contributions to the retirement plan. It was a great coup. She was a natural organizer and got great satisfaction from using this skill to help others.

When Karen moved to her new community, she was on the lookout for a way to use these organizing skills. She became interested in The Blue Zones, a health-oriented lifestyle organization. A little over a decade ago, *National Geographic*, partnering with writer Dan Buettner, discovered five regions of the world where people live measurably longer and better than elsewhere, attaining 100 years of age at 10 times greater rates than Americans. The researchers called these areas the Blue Zones. Teams of scientists traveled there and worked on identifying which of the inhabitants' lifestyle characteristics might explain their extraordinary longevity. After a bestselling series of books detailing the outcome, entitled *The Blue Zones* and *Thrive*, among others, they began an experiment to see whether these lifestyle choices could be introduced to, and adopted by, communities within the United States.

It was a perfect match for Karen. "Why not see how many people in my building might also be interested?" she thought to herself. She talked to the building leadership and put up signs. She called the new friends she had made and asked them to spread the word. On the night of the introductory meeting, she waited rather apprehensively in the community's social center. Outside, the weather was steamy and it was pouring rain. But people began to trickle in, and soon the room was filled to capacity. The concept proved to be a hit: her building adopted the lifestyle challenges, and since then she has introduced the organization to the other buildings in her community as well. "The excitement of building toward something important" has fueled further successes. Their building was the first approved by The Blue Zones organization in her area. "We are the leaders in that!" she said proudly.

What drives us in youth is often what gives us energy and perseverance in later life too. As a child in Sacramento, Joseph loved nature; when he was little he used to puzzle over the purple moon and how it got to be that color. He wanted to know how the world worked, especially the fascinating and infinitely complex relationship between man and nature. "I loved the effort to try to understand the life process," he said. "I had the realization that one can never know everything. It was so exciting."

Joseph spent most of his career studying cell life-cycles and the impact on disease replication. But "along the way I got asked to do other things," he said, and it was these things that became a driving force as he entered his 70s, wound down his travel schedule, and began to look for new activities to galvanize him.

"I got into a lot of other things that were relevant or derivative of my experience and knowledge and yet are not the same thing at all," he explained. These led him to the work that now consumes him. Years ago, for instance, he traveled to Tibet for work and became interested in land management and protection. He was involved in successfully petitioning the Chinese government to designate four million acres of land to remain undeveloped; that number has since risen to nine million. He now dedicates the majority of his time to being on the Board of the environmental organization that shepherded this transformation, and he describes his involvement in this organization over the last 30 years as "the single most important piece of my work."

"I'm 100% convinced of its importance, so it's pretty easy for me to commit to working in this realm. The way I'm spending my time now is very important to me," he said. Driven by a desire to use his wits to ensure our planet remains healthy, he works in an entirely different rhythm today than he did during the heyday of his career, but he finds that his sense of commitment and drive is just the same.

A new passion for altruism

But there isn't always a path to follow that seems obvious or easy, given past experiences. Our interviewees sometimes surprised themselves by their capacity to discover a new passion in something entirely unexpected.

There is a small, private boarding school close to the ocean in the town where Henry now lives, in the greater Los Angeles area. He moved to the community after his children were already grown, and other than recognizing the name of the school, he knew virtually nothing about it. One day, chatting with the contractor who was putting some finishing touches on his new home, he asked for advice: how could he become more involved in his new community? That's when he first heard about the school on whose behalf he now works tirelessly—sitting on the Board, raising money, and participating in long-term strategic decisions.

What spurred him to such dedication? He was impressed by the school's community-building gestures, which include leasing a small beach to the town for just $1 a year so the townspeople can have easy access to the ocean. He admires the school's diversity, its model for education, and the fact that it supports so many students with generous financial-aid packages. "It's one of my joys, to give them money," he said. Though he had never before been involved in educational philanthropy, he realized that working with people he admired was highly motivating. "I promised myself when I retired [that] I would only spend time with people I could have fun with," he said. "I actually turned down various Board positions because I thought I wouldn't have fun, even though they would have been lucrative."

Henry's story of finding a new passion in the form of giving back was a recurring theme we heard from a number of our interviewees. As they approached their later years, they naturally began to think about how to use their resources to meaningfully impact and improve the world. Many interviewees were able to delve deeper into specific passions through mentoring, volunteering, or philanthropy because of the combination of financial security and increased spare time that age allowed them. It was clear, anecdotally, that these activities gave them great joy.

Taking time to explore creativity

A number of our interviewees found their purpose in creative pursuits, which they now had the time to cultivate. In our chapter about growth we met Raymond, who transitioned from his career in finance to roping cattle to learning the art of documentary filmmaking in order to create a film about his high school class.

The success and joy that Raymond found in the film project awakened in him an interest in nurturing his creative side, and he decided to turn his attention to cultivating his long-held interest in photography. In keeping with the apprentice approach that had worked so well for him with cattle-roping and film-making, he hired a mentor—an expert photographer—from whom he could learn the many techniques and tools of the trade.

Now, almost four years on, his exploration of photography has blossomed into a vocation that occupies the majority of Raymond's time. He has built a studio in his house where he displays his work and has published two books chronicling his portfolio. He built a wooden display case to house the vintage cameras he has collected, which he uses to alter the effect of his shots, and he experiments with different types of paper for printing, finding challenge and enjoyment in adjusting the materials to capture just the right tone.

Although he loves to travel with his family, Raymond now also plans trips that he can take on his own, in order to spend dedicated time in one place, soaking in the atmosphere and taking photographs. In a few months he will head to Corsica, where he hopes the history and landscape will inspire him, and last year he spent a week in New York City, recording the variety of people he encountered on the streets. His interest in light, color, texture, and social dynamics has led him to a passion for capturing the essence of the people and communities he comes across.

The purpose he derives from this endeavor now shapes his days. He actively thinks about the next step—where he might go next, what new techniques he could learn, what details he could tweak—and each day he is driven to explore something new. "I think to myself: have I done enough? I guess it's good to have that drive. I don't want to wake up and be completely bored, but I don't want to have to be in five places [at once]. I want a balance between the two."

In Raymond's case, this seemingly wholly new life flourished from the seed of an interest that was already present. As he put it to us, "The artistic stuff has always been there." What changed was that he finally had the time and means to express this side of his personality to his full ability.

In later life, our interviewee Mary Jane, who is married to Walter, decided to try her hand at writing a memoir. Though she now lives in Scituate, Massachusetts, she grew up in 1950s Louisiana, a time and place she finds endlessly fascinating. For years she had dabbled halfheartedly at writing, taking classes and joining workshops, but she had never dedicated serious time and effort to completing an entire book. Once she had more freedom, she established a routine of sitting at her desk in front of her computer each and every Monday, Wednesday, and Friday morning from 8 a.m. till noon.

"It was great fun," she said. The routine allowed her to pare down the other activities in her life that were no longer providing her with as much enjoyment, and she managed to complete the entire book in less than a year. Mary Jane made a commitment to herself to work hard, and she thereby discovered the great satisfaction that comes from combining passion with effort.

Slowing down allows for deeper connections

Many of our interviewees enjoyed an injection of energy when they adopted different responsibilities in an already familiar environment; often, this involved staying in place but moving at a different pace—one that worked for this later stage of life.

When Paul turned 70, about a decade ago, his deanship at the large university where he had capped his career in teaching medicine was winding down and he wondered whether he should cut down on his teaching commitment. Then he was offered a chair, and he accepted the job, intrigued. The position allowed him to continue to do his medical research while maintaining all of his relationships at the institution. "It's a tremendous opportunity to not feel cut off, cast adrift," he said. "This is very different than how it can sometimes be in the corporate world."

Now almost 80 years old, Paul is still extremely active, occupying an office at the medical school, mentoring students, attending conferences, and teaching. His position allows him to keep a constellation of interests in his life, and he doesn't consider himself retired but rather in a "decrescendo mode of fewer

obligations." He feels lucky to have had the chance to shift perspectives and slow down a bit while still maintaining the variety
of interactions that have been so motivating for him in the past.
He had been worried about how to stay involved, but found that
his concerns never came to fruition. "It's typical of the academic
world—if you've done a good job, they are very good to you," he
said. It turns out that academia has been "a wonderful place to
wind down."

A role in an academic institution has also been helpful to
another of our interviewees, Walter. Now 80, Walter has had an
active career at a major medical school in Boston, where for decades he ran his own lab and taught graduate students about im-
munology. Seven years ago, he shut his lab down but was still able
to continue teaching, running two courses at the medical school,
going to conferences, and writing articles to submit to medical
journals.

Throughout his career, Walter has enjoyed his interactions
with the students, especially when engaging with them about career planning and what makes them tick. Over the years, a number of students have been the sons and daughters of youngsters
he taught decades earlier. He says, "It is still very rewarding to be
able to help people" through his insights and medical knowledge.
Recently, he decided to nominate a colleague, who had also become a friend of his, for a professional honor; "I previously didn't
have time for this kind of thing, and now I do," he explained.

It is worth noting that our interviewees with academic careers were especially well set up to continue their engagement on
a professional level, while being able to slow down the level and
pace of their commitments. The academic setting seems to be a
particularly good one for aging: people enjoy continued esteem

from colleagues, have opportunities to interact with people of different ages and to mentor young people, and stay tapped into the advances in their field through conferences and visiting scholars. If you could design a career that closely approximated the "elder" role of ancient cultures, this one would be close!

The fruits of our labors

While some of our interviewees were able to find purpose easily once their work and/or parenting responsibilities abated, others had to experiment and try several things before finding the project or pursuit that really worked for them. But, as the medical studies show, the search for purpose at this later stage in life is a project worth investing in. In fact, having financial resources can be a significant plus here; our interviewees' stories were filled with examples of how they used their resources to facilitate their discovering a purpose that would sustain them through this phase of life—whether it was funding a relocation, in the case of George and Jean, or hiring a mentor, as Raymond did, to fast-track immersion in a hobby that has now become a vocation.

And their efforts paid off. Our interviewees remain excited about and committed to their chosen pursuits—whether paid or unpaid, full-time or part-time—regardless of age. They found ways to remain tapped into skills they could exploit, interests they could pursue, and volunteering activities that give them pleasure—the kind of enjoyment that is lasting and deeply felt. Even when their commitments seemed like "work," they discovered that the sense of purpose they felt was profoundly satisfying.

One of the questions that researchers use to assess whether people perceive purpose in life is to have them rate their level of agreement with this statement: "I sometimes feel as if I've done all there is to do in life."[39] The purpose-driven individual will strongly disagree with this statement. So, how you would rate yourself? And if you're not satisfied with your answer, begin today to think how you might develop a purpose that will be worth living for.

CHAPTER FIVE
BEING PROACTIVE

....

Practical Steps for Allocating Resources in Later Life

Hopefully, you've gotten to this point and are feeling like you are well on your way to cultivating a successful and vibrant later life. You have agency, you have a growth mindset, you're engaged with others, and you are driven toward meaningful goals that give your life a sense of purpose and fulfillment. So, are you done? Can you check the box marked "Aging Well" and go home? Not quite yet. There is still the remaining, sometimes thorny issue of how you actually optimize the time you have left in this world. If you were to take a hard look at everything you are involved in, everything you pay for, and everything you spend time on, would you be satisfied with what you see? Would it be what you would choose if you could start from a blank slate today?

That is what this chapter is about. The truth is, if you have resources, you have the good fortune at this stage in life to be able to think creatively and imaginatively about how you would most like to spend those resources (both your time and money) and arrange your life accordingly. Yet many, if not most, people never fully embark on this process, instead letting inertia take hold.

They find themselves surrounded by the houses, possessions, activities, organizations, and lifestyles that may have made sense 10, 15, or even 20 years ago, but no longer suit their current realities.

This can be particularly true for highly successful people who are accustomed to operating in a state of constant forward momentum. It takes a proactive process of stepping back and pressing pause on this momentum to do the type of self-reflection required to examine your life and clarify your goals. And then it takes discipline and persistence to move toward those goals and to taper your commitment to parts of your life that no longer make sense or fit who you are now. This process can be challenging at any stage of life, but it can be even more emotionally fraught at later stages, when leaving aspects of life behind may trigger a sense of loss. The antidote to this sense of loss is having something fun to move toward. In this chapter we share what we learned from our interviewees about how they prioritized their time and used their financial resources to give them the most joy.

A more conscious allocation of "assets"

In his book *On the Shortness of Life*, the Roman philosopher Seneca wrote, "It is not that we have a short time to live but that we waste a lot of it. Life is long enough, and a sufficiently generous amount has been given to us for the highest achievements, if it were all well invested… So it is: we are not given a short life, but we make it short, and we are not ill-supplied but wasteful of it… Life is long if you know how to use it."[40]

As Seneca understood, life unfolds whether we choose how to spend it or not. So wouldn't it be better to choose proactively how to allocate our most precious assets—our time, energy, and resources? A comparison to asset allocation in the investment world seems apt. Consider all the time and expense devoted to arriving at the ideal asset allocation: how much money should be invested in stocks, bonds, alternatives, and so on. From an investment perspective, this is time well spent: studies have shown that the majority of investment results flow from this decision alone. Now what about the assets that are truly the most valuable in terms of the meaning and impact of our lives—our time, how we devote our energy, and how we think about all that might be accomplished through our resources? How much time do we devote to studying how to allocate those?

With financial resources comes the gift of actually having choices in this matter. Seize this freedom, and allocate the time to think meaningfully and deeply about how you will use these precious assets in your own life. If you were looking back in 10 years, would you be happy with the decisions you are making now? What type of life do you want to design for yourself and lead over the next 10 years? What impact do you want to have? If you feel constrained, ask yourself why—what is stopping you?

Business writer and Harvard professor Clayton Christensen has spent decades researching innovation and motivation. "With every moment of your time, every decision about how you spend your energy and your money, you are making a statement about what really matters to you," he writes. "Because if the decisions you make about where you invest your blood, sweat, and tears are not consistent with the person you aspire to be, you'll never become that person."[41]

Understanding and taking control of time

So, how do you become more purposeful in using the time you have? Our interviewee Lawrence, now 66 and beginning to contemplate what lies ahead, has been most influenced by his father's approach to life, which included a zest for living each moment fully, no matter how large or small. We asked Lawrence where people go wrong when they age. "Not being deliberate in their choices," he answered. "If you don't know (or care) where you are going, any road will do."

One way to become more deliberate is to work with someone who can help you gain perspective on what is really valuable to you. After her mother died, Peggy felt she needed help figuring out how to make important decisions about how to spend her time. A task-oriented person, she was focused on getting things done and often found herself engaged in activities that ate up enormous swaths of time, yet left her feeling empty. She decided to work with a coach. "I started at that point trying to acknowledge and integrate, and really trust and value, my intuition to a greater extent than I ever had before," she said. After working with a number of coaches over the years, Peggy feels she has learned not only how to prioritize her time but also how to play to her strengths when figuring out what to spend her time on. "I was learning to be bolder about who I was and what my strengths were," she said.

Psychologist and author Mary Pipher describes going through a similar thought process in her book *Another Country*. Struck with the observation that "As people age, time, not money, becomes real wealth," she embarked upon a process when she turned 50 to clarify what was important to her and invented a mnemonic device, the Five R's, to help her keep track of her

priorities: respect, relationships, results, relaxation, and realization. She describes how she uses the mnemonic this way: "Since
then, I have tried to use the Five R's to budget my time. When
I have choices to make, I ask 'Will this project bring me what I
want? Will this decision make me more relaxed or respected? Will
it bring results in the culture or for those I love?' If the answer is
no, I try to turn down activities and projects. I try to make every
minute matter. There is time for only the Five R's."[42]

When time is at a premium, it makes sense to experience it
more fully. Sometimes people make the valid choice not to in-
sist that every moment be spent in a way that leads to specific,
quantifiable outcomes—rather, they choose to dwell in the moment and truly savor it. Buddhist writer and philosopher Lewis
Richmond calls this concept "'vertical time,' which means this
present moment: this room, this book, this body, this breath."[43]
It is a concept of time as something more still than a linear series
of clearly defined, sequential events. "In contrast to a vehicle on
the highway of horizontal time," he says, "vertical time is like a
house resting on a foundation. It is solid."[44] One of the advantages of perceiving time differently in later life is that, rather than
feeling older and seeing ourselves on the far right of the historical
continuum of our lives, we can instead feel both fully present and
open to possibility. Lewis explains, "When we include vertical
time—the timeless conviction of the present moment—we can
find relief from the signposts on horizontal time's highway."[45]

Several of our interviewees shared stories with us that seemed
very similar to this notion of vertical time. When Henry was a
child growing up in rural California, he was always on the go.
Compelled to try every activity and participate in every party,
he often felt frazzled but was happy nonetheless. He would go

from playing cards with friends to riding horses, from doing the paper route to signing up for the after-school debate team. He remembers one day in particular, when he was squirreled away in his room intently focused on an activity, having just finished another project moments earlier. His father lingered in the doorway, studying him, and then advised him to savor time more fully instead of always rushing through it.

"My father used to say, 'Don't wish your life away,' because I was always in a hurry to get somewhere," Henry explained. "And now I have the time…and I say, 'I better not be wishing away my time.' So my philosophy of life is living more in the present. Pause and smell the roses. I used to be in such a hurry to get out the door in the morning, to get to work or travel, that I didn't even notice the weather other than if I had to wear a jacket or not… Now it's about being more conscious of what's going on, on a sensory level."

One day recently, he was pulling out of the driveway on his way to a dentist appointment. "I literally had time to look at four deer that were in the meadow by my house," he said. "I was looking at the natural elegance of the deer—it was kind of fun." His slower pace allows him to fully participate in these small pleasures of life, which has the effect of making each moment feel richer.

Staving off regret

Whether optimizing time or savoring every moment, the key seems to be spending time in a way that will minimize later regret about how you have used this precious resource. If you could look back 10 years from now, would you be happy with how you spent the time you had?

This framework of minimizing regret is very close to the approach that George Kinder, one of the founders of the "life planning" movement in financial advising, uses in his work with clients. Kinder's approach centers on helping clients discover their "deepest and most profound goals through a process of structured and non-judgmental inquiry."[46] He does this by asking clients three simple questions:

1. How would you live your life if you were financially secure?

2. If you had only 5 to 10 years to live, what would you do in the time you have remaining?

3. If you were informed that you had only 24 hours to live, what would you feel? What would you miss? Who did you not get to be? What did you not get to do?

We have used these three questions in our work with clients and find that they, more than most goal-defining exercises we've come across, have a way of shining a clear light on whether people feel good about how they are allocating their time—particularly the last question, which often awakens in people the type of regret they might experience if they were to leave certain things undone in life. The question alerts people to parts of themselves that they may not yet have expressed and areas of life that they need to reprioritize. There is more to the process that Kinder recommends, which ultimately helps individuals shape their futures (especially how they allocate their time and money) so they align with their reprioritized vision, but we have found that even simply answering these three questions can provide a watershed moment of clarity. It's suddenly very evident whether you are spending your time in the right place.

So much of time management is about prioritization—keeping the important stuff while minimizing the superfluous. Sometimes our interviewees found that by dedicating time proactively toward an activity they valued, they by default minimized the time available for less fulfilling activities. Our interviewee Mary Jane, whom we met earlier when she explained how she had found renewed purpose in life by choosing to prioritize her writing, explained to us how she made time to stick to the discipline that this new goal required of her. "Like many others, I'm committed to many things," she said. But deciding to dedicate three mornings a week to writing gave her the impetus—almost the license—to weed out other, extraneous activities. "It allowed me to give up a good many things that I didn't want to pick up again," she said.

Though she had always been active in her local church—she had served as senior warden and run the welcoming committees for years—Mary Jane now felt it was time to move on. "Frankly, I felt like I'd given my gift, and I didn't want to continue doing it at that level anymore. I was very happy when I did it, and then I was done." Another critical element that helped her focus more purposefully on activities she valued was deciding to be less flexible with her time. "I cut out being available to everyone all the time and continued to do only the things that I liked to do," she said.

Mary Jane's experience gets to the heart of the issue. It's easy to mistake being busy with being intentionally engaged in things you find fulfilling and that will matter to you in the long run. This can be a hard balance to strike. Busyness in its own right can be satisfying day to day, and, particularly during periods of transitions, it can be a welcome antidote to a sense of loss, of no longer being needed at work or at home. Yet, over time, being busy does not necessarily equate to being fulfilled. As you reflect on how to best use your time, think about this balance in your life and whether it's sufficiently tilted toward meaning to stave off any regrets your future self might have.

Putting financial resources to best use

Once you have done the work of evaluating whether you are spending your time in the right place, the next task is to think about the optimal use of your financial resources. As wealth advisors, we are immersed in this area, seeing our clients' uses of their wealth and observing which seem to produce the most lasting satisfaction and the least unintended consequences.

It was clear from our discussions that, almost without noticing, all of our interviewees were using their financial resources as a tool to invest in their ability to experience the four factors of positive aging: to be the agents of their own destiny; to learn new things and reinvent themselves; to open doors that allow them to forge relationships with people from other walks of life; to feed a curious, learning mind through mentored apprenticeship or travel; and, overall, to provide the financial security that allows them to donate their time and energy to causes they find rich and fulfilling.

Specifically, we heard from our interviewees that they found seven ways of using their financial resources to be particularly valuable in achieving positive aging. We describe them here:

1. **Arranging family experiences:** Many interviewees found pleasure in hosting or otherwise enabling their families to spend time together. Judy invites her extended family to her house in Newport, where everyone loves

to swim in the ocean and picnic on the lawn. Donald enables his two daughters and their partners to join him and his wife in the Caribbean each year; he rents a villa and pays all their expenses. "If you pay for food, planes, lodging, they will come!" he said, grinning. Joyce and her husband chose to buy a vacation home close to New York City so that their children and young grandchildren could easily jump on a train and visit. "It's more of a gift for us than it is for them," Joyce said. "I mean, we love our family, and we want to spend time with them." Everyone cooks together in the big kitchen and sits together by the lake, keeping life low-key. "We couldn't do it if we didn't have the money," she added.

2. **Supporting education:** Having resources in later years allows people to support their children's and grandchildren's educations, which is consistently a source of great satisfaction. Karen, who co-ran a company with her husband in Philadelphia, always put a premium on education. Her three children were high achievers, and she and her husband paid for their undergraduate and graduate degrees. Now she has seven grandchildren, the youngest of whom has special needs. They follow an 80/20 rule, in which she and her husband provide up to 80% of the financial support for education that a grandchild needs. Because of their financial support, their youngest grandchild has been able to get physical therapy and have a specialized tutor. Similarly, George and Jean have put their nieces and nephews through college—13 children total—and set up a fund in Jean's high school to help 35 teens pay for college.

3. **Traveling adventurously:** We have already seen that experiencing foreign places and meeting different people contributes to continued learning and vastly enriches life. Donald, the business school professor, said, "Our lives are very simple right now. We don't live very extravagantly except for our vacations." His next trip is to Tanzania and Uganda. George and Jean take active trips together all over the world, and Diane uses her funds to underwrite annual art-themed trips that take her from Amsterdam to Morocco to Tibet and back. Many of our interviewees used trips as opportunities to invite family members along, or to nurture friendships with people all over the world. Being able to be mobile and nimble gives them a chance to explore, immerse themselves in novel perspectives, stretch their minds, and share with others.

4. **Giving to meaningful causes:** We saw earlier that when people feel passionately about a topic or action, it fuels their sense of drive. Many of our interviewees derive tremendous satisfaction from financially supporting the cause they are most passionate about. Joseph spends so much of his time managing and supporting environmental projects that he is busier now than when he was working full-time as a biologist. As she ages, Judy has increasingly felt happier giving money away than spending it. "Generosity is something we can indulge in now," she said with a big smile.

5. **Maintaining health:** The majority of our interviewees spend considerable money on healthcare—by purchasing concierge care for themselves or their relatives, for

example. This gives them peace of mind; they expressed gratitude and relief that while they might face physical or mental deterioration, they never need to worry about paying for the best care available.

6. **Hiring an advisor:** It is a privilege not to have to sweat the details, and many of our interviewees have been happy to trust others with managing their wealth and all of the implications of that wealth within their families. "I never really think about it anymore," said Raymond. "It has freed me up to focus on all the other things I love. I don't worry about my kids anymore and how they're relating to the money and so on." This was a common sentiment. Perhaps not surprisingly, none of our interviewees said that they derived much satisfaction or meaning from managing their wealth—in fact, it was just the opposite. They expressed gratitude that they do not have to worry about the wealth management process anymore and that they have been freed up to figure out how to use their money as the tool it is—a means to an end (i.e. a fulfilling, engaged later life), rather than the end in itself.

7. **Allowing little indulgences:** Last but not least, some explained that with age had come the realization that they would have more than enough money to support themselves comfortably for the rest of their lives, and that this realization had given them newfound license to indulge in little extras that their younger, more frugal selves would have avoided. Margo, now 81, said she had always been conservative with her finances but that she has recently begun to rethink her relationship to money.

She and her husband had always owned their cars and kept them for many years. But when her old Volvo died, she thought to herself for the first time: "Why shouldn't I have what I really want?"—and she got herself a new car with all the bells and whistles. While it wasn't a huge indulgence in the grand scheme, the ability to get those little perks without a shred of guilt was a new feeling for Margo.

From wealth creator to wealth consumer

We also explored with our interviewees how their conceptions of their wealth had evolved over time. Not surprisingly, the psychological transition for affluent, successful older people from "wealth creator" to "wealth consumer" (or "wealth steward") can be tricky. If the score-keeping aspect of wealth accumulation makes a person happy, it can often be difficult to transition away from this mentality, particularly when money not only no longer comes in but also begins to go out.

Judy was eloquent about how her relationship with the idea of accumulation has changed over the years: "I think the concept of 'enough' is also very important for those of us who have made it this long," she said. "When does one say that you have 'enough' and let go of some of the 'shoulds' and 'musts' that were pushing us along at an earlier age? To age gracefully, I think, you have to let go of some of those turbo-charged imperatives that were part of earlier types of success."

Judy's wisdom cuts to the heart of an issue that we see a number of clients struggle with as they pass through different stages of life. Many of our clients come to us in mid-life, when they are naturally busy with their careers and focused on wealth accumulation and the tax planning that leads to wealth preservation. There is often a form of score-keeping, with progress measured in a growing balance sheet or a strong quarterly investment return. But the score-keeping metrics that serve clients well during this accumulation phase cease to be as relevant or motivating later in life, as people start to think more deeply about the purpose of the wealth and ask themselves, "What is all this money for?"

Margo, the former schoolteacher, used to keep score by gauging how much money was coming in and how much was going out. This was less about saving money than about maintaining a sense of control. Now she often asks herself, "Will it really matter in the long run?" She has a friend who spends hours analyzing her monthly heat bill, despite being financially comfortable. To Margo, this seems like energy directed in the wrong place; she would rather focus on the new and interesting activities she can undertake with the extra time she has.

But it can be a difficult emotional transition; it can feel like giving up or letting things go unattended, when really it is a realigning of focus to hone in on what is important now. At a recent conference on the impact of wealth, the attendees discussed what it takes for someone to make the move from the accumulation phase to this next, more reflective phase. "It requires the abandonment of ego and a willingness to do that," said an entrepreneur at my table, who had just reached the milestone of his 60th birthday.

Some have described this change as a sort of awakening, often brought about by the birth of a grandchild or a similar event that changes a person's relationship to money. "I think I need to think less about making money now than about what I hope to do with all that I've made," said Donald, the business-school professor from Chicago. He remembers being told that life is really all about your children being healthy and happy, yet when he was driven to excel in business and succeed financially, he couldn't see it that way. "I used to think, 'This can't be all there is,'" he said, "but now I agree."

Our interviewee Michael says he is aware that it is all too easy to get stuck in a pattern of saving all your money and accumulating wealth rather than figuring out how to spend it wisely and in a way that brings you real happiness and meaning. "It becomes so habitual when you're in your 50s and 60s that you can't break out of it," he explained. However, once you recognize that money is a tool to be used thoughtfully, it gives you much more satisfaction. "Those greenbacks do have meaning, but they're not real. It's probably the greatest tool you'll ever have—not the greatest thing, but the greatest tool."

Often people struggle with this transition and remain stuck in old modes of thinking. "Money represents freedom," Michael said, "but it only becomes freeing if you view it freely. Think to yourself: why are you holding on to it?... It's only going to your kids if you don't spend it on yourself. I see money as a utility, to meet my own needs but also to help other people."

Sometimes the very activity or lifestyle that brought someone joy earlier ceases to play the same role later in their lives. As Raymond has grown older and delved with greater focus into his various artistic projects, he has started feeling the urge to simplify—to be less tied down, to have less stuff to manage: "My lifestyle has changed, and I ask myself, 'Do I really need this?' I want to be more flexible." Though he has valued the time with his family in Arizona, where he learned cattle roping, he wonders now whether it might be the moment to move on. He no longer wants the burden of taking care of too many properties; he would prefer to be nimble and adapt the use of his resources to what is most meaningful for him now.

Learning to let go

Committing to proactively direct your time, energy, and uses of wealth will inevitably require letting go of some things that no longer make the top of your list. We'll spend the next section hearing stories from our interviewees about how they managed the process of letting go. It was easier when they were leaving behind something they no longer valued or that they now prioritized differently. And it was also easier when there was something to go toward, when they were being pulled toward something they would rather do.

About four years ago, Raymond decided it was time to hand over the reins of his family's charitable foundation to his three children. He was spending more time on his photography and was deriving less enjoyment from the work involved in managing the foundation. "What are you holding on for?" he asked himself. "Do something else! If the kids can handle it, then why not let them do it?" He had always had confidence in his children, and his giving up the need to manage the foundation allowed them to feel truly empowered in this arena. "It's their life," he said. "They're adults. You can't continue to interject yourself in their lives unless you want to enable them."

Now, looking back, he feels that the positive repercussions of letting go—in terms of the growth in his own life and in the lives of his children—were much greater than if he had tried to maintain control. It was a valuable lesson that he had originally learned as a tank commander in Vietnam, where "you couldn't apply your standards in every situation, because people are so different." As a consequence of this early experience, his philosophy became less top-down and more egalitarian. He was willing to let his children execute on their own vision, and he was open-minded and agreed when his children proposed converting the foundation to a donor-advised fund in order to minimize the operational burden and allow them to focus on the part they most enjoyed, which was making the charitable donations. He summarized his philosophy as leading by example rather than needing to micromanage: "[Children] see you do these things," he said. "If you're doing something good, the children will see it; it's going to stick with them."

Our interviewee Karen shared a similar story of being willing to step back and let her children take on real responsibility for the family's philanthropic giving. Very early in her two children's lives, Karen started talking with them about eventually turning over responsibility for her family's foundation to them. She and her husband regularly took the children on site visits and even included them in some of the decision-making. "We learned about the charities together, and they felt very comfortable with it all," Karen said.

Her daughter Lily took the initiative early on: she was interested in an organization that teaches life skills to pre-teen girls, which Karen had never heard of. "Your child expresses interest, and then you become involved," Karen said, explaining that it was a two-way street. As Lily is very health-minded, she also wanted to try establishing vegetable gardens in an urban environment, and even though her efforts were not particularly successful, everyone learned something valuable from the experience. Eventually it became a family enterprise: once Lily grew older and got married, her husband also became involved. Although philanthropy was a new experience for him, he had always maintained an interest in tennis, and so he launched an after-school tennis program for young children. Now, he serves on a national Board.

When it comes to letting the next generation take over, "you just have to have an open mind," Karen said. "You have to decide what's more important: do I want to get what I want, or do I want them to be excited about philanthropy?" Letting go of the need to control ends up benefiting everyone: "We kind of let them lead the pack because we want them to be involved."

You are now on "a journey with several destinations"

In the wealth advising world, Raymond's and Karen's eager willingness to hand over the reins of the family endeavor to their children is not always the norm. One of the thorniest issues (and one of the most common that we see) in relation to the allocation of time and letting go is succession. It's rare that family patriarchs and matriarchs proactively and willingly cede control to the next generation. In fact, advisors who are hired by first-generation wealth holders are often asked to find increasingly elaborate ways to help the first generation maintain control. Yet it is often more effective to help the first generation step back sufficiently to respect—and even nurture—the next generation's need to experience real ownership and accountability.

In his book *Stewardship in Your Family Enterprise*, sociologist and author Dennis Jaffe, Ph.D., put it this way: "As life expectancy increases—and along with it the number of active years a person can look forward to—family leaders, like others in society, must begin to think of their lives not as a single ladder, but rather as a journey with several destinations. Business leadership may be one of the middle stages, so people need to develop a positive image of life beyond this and develop the motivation to achieve in the post business life stages."[47]

In order for this transition to go well, it's critical for the first generation to develop the capacities we discussed earlier in the book: to employ a learner's mind, a willingness to reinvent your identity, and an ability to let go. Lawrence told us that as he approached the prospect of turning over the reins of the business he founded to his younger colleagues, the predominant emotion he felt was fear—but that this fear was followed by intrigue and interest as he realized he would have to figure out how to reinvent himself. He would need to find new ways of spending his time, and this would not only open up possibilities for him but also give him a chance to get rid of the activities he didn't like. "Yes, there's fear," he told us, "but there are some very positive possibilities about the future. If only the fear had been there, then it would have been really hard to proceed."

As we saw with our interviewees, when people are able to push through their fears and accept change rather than resist it, they move from a control orientation to one that is more creative, expansive, and generative. They are able to step back from needing to control everything—and measuring success that way—and move toward empowering others to be in charge. This in turn lets them measure success by how smoothly the transition has gone and the level of ownership and agency that the next generation of leaders feels.

Judging from our interviewees, there can be joy, and even some relief, in that transition and the possibilities it creates. Henry told us that he actually experienced a sense of euphoria when he stopped being CEO. "The mantle of responsibility," as he put it, had been lifted off of him; and now, after years of always working for his customers, employees, and Board, he has more time for all of the things he loves and to just enjoy the "luxury of being able to think more broadly."

Similarly, Lawrence said that, while it hasn't always been easy, overall it has been a joy to see the management of what he built successfully transition to the younger colleagues whom he has mentored for years. "The best use I can think of for it [the company] is to pass it on to my younger colleagues, so that is what I am in the process of doing. Watching my colleagues develop and grow into their expanding responsibilities has been very gratifying."

A conscious focus on goals and values—often in partnership

Each story we have shared in this chapter arose from the goals and personalities of the interviewees who lived them, combined with their actual efforts to turn their desires from abstractions into reality. Given your personal preferences and past experiences, what can you do to be more proactive about embracing this later phase of life?

The first step is to clarify your priorities and figure out whether you are living in a way that reflects them. How close are you to the life you want? Are you allocating your time, energy, and

resources to the things that matter to you most? In thinking this
through, consider your:

- personal and professional relationships
- location
- possessions
- health and well-being
- career/work/volunteering
- money
- and hobbies/interests

Your approach will change depending on whether you are
making decisions on your own or with a life partner. Many of
our interviewees expressed deep contentment with their spouses,
while also acknowledging that they and their partner did not always see eye to eye on goals or have the same way of getting to a
shared outcome.

Our interviewee Henry, from the LA area, told us how much
he enjoys working from home now, especially since it means he
can have breakfast with his wife, Grace, whom he calls his best
friend. Of course there are some challenges to sharing the space—
like when Grace practices scales on the piano, Henry tells us with
a laugh. But in general they've worked out a system in which
they give each other the latitude both to have time together and
to pursue their own interests. Henry does his work and reads;
Grace takes Pilates, attends a book club, and learns Portuguese by
Skyping with a teacher in London. On a macro level, they have
agreed on what makes them happy—how much to work, whether
to stay in California, and so on—while on a micro level, they have
worked out a nice balance between time alone and time together.

Raymond operates in partnership with his wife when they discuss the possibility of shifting priorities and downsizing. Asked which personal circumstances have the most effect on the aging process, he answered first that working in concert with your spouse is critical. "You have to have a life that fits two people's desires," he said. This can mean managing differences in age and personal goals—and figuring out how to negotiate goals that might be conflicting. "Approach this process with an open mind, a positive attitude, honesty and a willingness to listen from a different perspective, and you may discover things you never realized about yourself and your partner," write Roberta Taylor and Dorian Mintzer in *The Couple's Retirement Puzzle*. "Remember that creating a vision for what you both want in the next part of your life is a process that begins with small steps and evolves over time."[48]

You are your next investment

We have found that the key to success at this stage is viewing yourself as your next investment, by arranging your life so that your time, energy, and wealth are all being directed toward activities that give you the most meaning and satisfaction. Deciding how to spend your time and energy is a multi-step process, and it is often helpful to work on it with a person who can guide you, whether a financial advisor or another type of coach.

Here are some tactics we have seen work well in our consultations with clients:

- Enlist a coach, advisor, or friend to help you through this process.

- First work through the brainstorming and envisioning on your own, and then discuss it with your spouse or partner.

- Articulate the vision you are aiming for—it helps to lay out the dream, so to speak.

- Hold yourself accountable. Either review your plan annually or ask your coach or advisor to hold you accountable for bringing these goals to life.

It is all too easy for daily life to get in the way of fully engaging with this process. Our advice is to use to your advantage the opportunity you have to make choices and to understand that the process of moving toward the goals you really want may necessitate letting go of what currently occupies your time. Often, when lack of time is the reason for not tackling what you really want to do, the true culprit is those activities that continue to weigh on you past the point where they are fulfilling.

Truth is, as we have learned, seeing this stage of life as an opportunity to assess and reengage opens up all sorts of new possibilities. "As long as we keep comparing ourselves to a younger, better self (who may have been better only in hindsight), we shortchange the possibilities for becoming an older, wiser one," writes Lewis Richmond, author of *Aging as a Spiritual Practice*. "The wisdom of Adaptation begins in the willingness to let go of who we used to be and embrace who we are now."[49]

Questions to help you evaluate how to spend your resources now

1. Am I making assumptions about how I wish to spend my time and money? Have I reassessed my goals recently?

    ....
    ....
    ....

2. If I had only five years to live, what would I want to spend my time doing?

    ....
    ....
    ....
    ....

3. If I were told that tomorrow would be my last day on this earth, what would I most regret not having done? Who did I not get to be?

    ....
    ....
    ....

4.   What did I dream of doing when I was a young child?

....

....

....

....

....

5.   In the midst of a busy life of work and responsibilities, what did I yearn to do the most?

....

....

....

....

6.   When, in the past month or two, did I have the experience of "flow" while undertaking an activity? What was it about the activity that led me to experience this state of being?

....

....

....

....

7.   What are the responsibilities and activities occupying
      my time that give me the least pleasure?

....

....

....

....

8.   If I am resisting change at work or at home, what is
      it I am really afraid of?

....

....

....

....

....

9.   What do I really want, as opposed to what I think I
      should want?

....

....

....

....

....

10.   Are there expenses in my life that could be put to
       better use, now that I am older?

....

....

....

11.   When I look at all of the assets (homes, possessions)
       on my balance sheet, do I feel that this use of my
       resources is well-aligned with what would give me
       the most joy and fulfillment today?

....

....

....

....

....

12.   How might I allocate my resources in such a way as
       to allow me to cultivate the four factors in aging well:
       agency, growth, engagement, and drive?

....

....

....

....

SECTION TWO

The Gift of Clarity

....

Contemplating Your Last Years—For Your Own
Good and That of Your Family

Hopefully, by this point you're feeling inspired by all of the vibrant possibilities that later life presents. You might even be wondering whether you need to read Section Two—with all of these positive stories of aging and a roadmap to get you started on your own journey of becoming gracefully AGED, what more is there to discuss?

It turns out there is one more very critical topic that we need to address if we are going to talk seriously about aging well. It's how to make sure that when you leave the earth, you like what you've left behind, in terms of how your loved ones will remember you and your life and how they will think of you when they consider the impact that your aging and death (and all of its ancillary repercussions, like putting your estate plan into motion) had on their lives. If Section One was mostly about the quality of life that you will have as you get older, this section is primarily about the impact that your later life and aging will have on others.

You may feel like you've heard this before and that you are all set on this front. After all, much of the work of the wealth advising profession centers on helping parents structure bequests that will define their legacy for their children or support their philanthropic goals. But we're not talking about the money you will leave behind. We're talking about the meaning. The lasting gift that brings true peace of mind to children is the gift of clarity: What did Dad or Mom want us to do with this money? Why did our parents structure their plan in this way? What kind of care does Mom want? Did I manage to fully honor Dad's wishes in his last days?

Providing clarity by itself is not hard. It can be accomplished in one or two family meetings or even in a letter. What is hard is the mental and emotional work that you have to go through to get to sufficient clarity in your own thoughts to be in a position to communicate clearly to your loved ones. It takes concentrated attention and effort, not to mention a willingness to face the fact that you will not live forever. As a result, it often goes unattended to until it's too late.

Our last book, *Raised Healthy, Wealthy & Wise*, centered on the challenges parents face when they try to strike the difficult balance between wanting to help their children but not wanting to enable or demotivate them. Interestingly, clarity turns out to be one of the few examples of a gift that has only upside in the life of the child. Think of two children, one who understands what his parents were trying to communicate through their estate plan, who understands his parents' wishes for their care at the end of their lives, and who knows the way in which his parents hope to leave this world; then think of another who is in the dark on all of these matters. Which child would you rather be? Almost all of us would choose to be the first—but, based on how rarely these conversations occur, almost all of us will be the second. Worse yet, we will impart this fate on our own children unless we commit to doing the work that this section covers.

There are several areas that really need to be addressed, where children seek information and guidance from a parent: understanding the rationale behind estate planning decisions; understanding parents' priorities regarding healthcare and living arrangements; and knowing parents' wishes for their death experiences. When parents do not communicate about these issues, children come to regret that they did not have the courage to ask before it was too late. Children may live for years with unanswered questions, resentment toward a sibling over unexplained estate planning decisions, or guilt and worry over having guessed at how a parent wanted their last days and moments to unfold.

But the good news is you truly can do the work to make sure this is not how your children will feel. It's a surmountable obstacle, with a clear path to results. In some ways, it's simpler than a lot of the problems we see in our work, as long as you are willing to put in the effort.

So how do you get started? That is what this section is about. This is the kind of thinking that cannot be outsourced, but you can get help—and that is our aim. For each area, we will show you what you need to think about and decide, plus offer questions to ask yourself to clarify your own thinking before attempting to share it with others. We will talk about what needs to be communicated and why, and tell stories of how other people have done this. Our goal is to give you concrete ideas that you can apply today, for your benefit and that of your family. And to help you get started, now, while you can!

CHAPTER SIX

THE POWER OF SHARING STORIES

Communicating Family Stories, Values, and the Meaning Behind Your Estate Plan

When people contemplate their legacies, they tend to think of what they will leave behind physically: properties, investments, artwork, books, photos, cars—the tangible. Naturally, they hope and expect that their values—which are far more nebulous and hard to define—will also be passed on to those they love and will continue living beyond their own physical presence in the world. But why leave this to chance? Each of us has a store of precious treasures inside our heads: unshared memories that no one else in the world can ever know; the unique values that guide pivotal choices in our lives; heartfelt messages that only we can share with loved ones; and the deeper reasons behind critical estate planning decisions we've made.

Why not take the steps to make sure these gifts are transferred to those you love after your death, just as you might leave behind a valued photograph or a favorite necklace? Why not devote as much time to articulating and passing down these intangibles as you would to planning the concrete, legal aspects of your estate plan? They are as important, if not more so.

The largest study ever conducted around legacy issues interviewed 2,627 baby boomers and elders and found that, in fact, children view the non-financial aspects of their parents' legacy (values, life-lessons, family stories) as 10 times more important than any financial inheritance. Yet the study also found that, while 68% of the elder generation agreed with the statement "It is my responsibility to initiate a conversation with my children about my legacy," only 31% of those surveyed felt that a comprehensive legacy discussion had occurred within their own families.[50]

Our goal with this chapter is to turn those statistics around. Ultimately, this chapter is about staving off regret—the regret of having left things unsaid, of allowing family stories to be lost forever or conflict to fester over estate planning decisions you might have explained during your life.

We'll take them one at a time and use story-telling as the unifying framework. These are your stories to tell, and only you can tell them.

Your unique memories matter

In our previous book, *Raised Healthy, Wealthy & Wise*, it became ever clearer to us that our successful inheritors had a deep knowledge of family that helped them develop a healthy relationship to money. Without that grounding, they risked getting lost in the empty habit of spending money and the agony of not knowing their own roles in the world. A 2001 Emory University study revealed that children who knew more about their family's history had a stronger sense of control over their lives, as well as healthier self-esteem and a greater belief in the strength and integrity of their families. The first study was conducted before the devastation of 9/11; a follow-up survey, after the disaster, revealed that those children who knew more about their families were more resilient than those who knew less, and could handle the effects of stress more effectively. [51]

In 2013, *The Atlantic* analyzed a number of studies on storytelling and also concluded that the practice confers significant benefits to listeners. "In the preteen years, children whose families collaboratively discuss everyday events and family history more often have higher self-esteem and stronger self-concepts," wrote professor Elaine Reese. "And adolescents with a stronger knowledge of family history have more robust identities, better coping skills, and lower rates of depression and anxiety. Family storytelling can help a child grow into a teen who feels connected to the important people in her life."[52]

People have a tendency to underestimate the importance of sharing the foundational memories of their lives, whether the powerful ones or the most mundane, often questioning whether they are even relevant in the modern age. But the truth is that sharing these stories is far less about you than it is about the younger generations who will follow you. Once those memories are gone, they can never be retrieved.

David O'Neil runs Story Trust, which interviews people about their lives and then captures and shares their stories with family and others through audio recordings and written memoirs. He came upon this career in a purely personal way. Having grown up in a large family with five siblings, he had always participated in big family gatherings where stories were bandied about over the dinner table. "But some were untold or half told," he said. Since he was born into this culture, he took it for granted, thinking he knew a lot about his family—when in reality "children know so little about their parents, it's really remarkable."

In his mid-20s, when David was courting his wife, he was trying to explain his family history and culture to her when it dawned on him how little he really understood about where he came from. Yes, there were aunts who had researched the family's genealogy ("binders and binders of dead people," as he put), but no one had unearthed the stories. David wanted to understand his parents more deeply—their lives as children, as teenagers, as a young couple—yet he had never thought to ask what their experiences had been like. He had two basic questions: (1) Who am I, and to what extent did my family define who I am? (2) Who are my parents as people, as individuals? His mother, then 77 years old, agreed to sit down with him and they arranged to do an interview at the end of the summer. David bought recording equipment and thought up a series of questions, and then—just as he was poised to record her—she fell and broke her hip, entering the hospital. Two weeks later she passed away. David had missed his chance, just barely.

He recalled a picture that he treasures of his mother as a young woman, perched in a bathing suit on the hood of a car: "She was looking sassy, a pack of cigarettes tucked in her waistband. I was thinking, 'That woman is not my mother.' I wanted to know who she was, and I never will… I was within a hair's breadth, but I missed it!"

The positive impact of sharing personal stories

In 2003, a small booth with some basic recording equipment

was erected in Grand Central Terminal in New York City. The idea was to capture passersby's stories—a kind of revival of the tradition of oral storytelling, whose purpose was to share wisdom among family members, generations, or different cultures. Within 10 years, this effort—now called StoryCorps—expanded to include five books, regular broadcasts on National Public Radio, and an app for use on mobile devices.

"We do this to remind one another of our shared humanity, to strengthen and build the connections between people, to teach the value of listening, and to weave into the fabric of our culture the understanding that everyone's story matters," states the non-profit's website. "At the same time, we are creating an invaluable archive for future generations." Two surveys, conducted online and through NPR, revealed that listeners felt sharing personal stories had benefits even beyond recording personal histories, including reminding them of their shared humanity (81%); helping them see the value in everyone's life story and experience (80%); humanizing social issues, events, and policies (80%); making them think about how society could be improved (71%); and making them feel more positive about society (70%).[53]

But despite these larger benefits and a younger generation eager to hear their elders' family stories, it can take some coaxing to encourage an older member of the family to actually take the proactive step to be interviewed. We talked to David about the objections he typically hears and how he overcomes them.

"I don't have much of a story to tell—nothing exciting ever happened in our family."
Response: Who will tell the story, whatever it is, if not you? You know more than anyone else, and today's mundane details are tomorrow's treasured history.

"This seems too egotistical: a whole interview about me and my thoughts?"

Response: It doesn't have to be about you. Focus on the stories of your parents and grandparents—those who came before you. Tell their story before it's lost forever.

"I don't want to recall painful moments."

Response: This is understandable. In memoir (versus autobiography), you are free to tell the story as you remember it and focus only on the parts you want to share. Don't miss telling the family story altogether just to avoid sharing a few select parts.

"Being asked to recollect my life story makes me feel like my life is over."

Response: This is a work in progress! Let's start now, while you're healthy and willing. We can always add more.

"I'm self-conscious. What will my family think of what I say?"

Response: Families are almost universally grateful to have the stories captured and almost always learn something new and valuable.

The bottom line is that the process of capturing an elder's story doesn't typically happen by default. Someone has to ask. And when someone does, the benefits are palpable. As David says, "For the storyteller, the process can have really profound effects. They gain insights into their lives, they learn something new about their lives, they synthesize their thoughts about the meaning of events in their lives."

David told us the story of Jane. In her 80s when David met

her, Jane was a strong and determined woman whose youngest
son had been born with Down Syndrome in the 1960s. While it
was expected that he would be institutionalized, Jane refused, raising her son at home and working with other parents to form an
advocacy group for children with intellectual handicaps. "When
we finished her book, Jane told me how much it meant to her to
have her story told and shared with her family," David said.

After Jane's memoir was completed, one of her granddaugh-
ters turned seven and was beginning to read. Every night at the
dinner table, Jane's granddaughter would read from the book
about her grandmother's life. Jane's family could see her conviction and courage brought to life, and the impact on Jane—not
only knowing her story was captured for posterity, but also seeing
it help shape her granddaughter's values and sense of compassion
in real time—was profound.

The positive effect on the storytellers extends even to those
who might have already begun to experience age-related mental
decline. In his book *How We Age*, Dr. Marc Agronin analyzes the
effect that telling stories and digging up memories has on the
most vulnerable elderly—those already beginning to suffer from
memory loss. "It is tempting to view these long-term memories as
permanently shaped channels in the brain, but research indicates
that they are more malleable than previously thought," he writes.
The very process of recollection can be healing: "When recalled,
memories become like softened gels that are then remembered or
consolidated back to their hardened forms by neurons that reacti-
vate the connections between them."[54]

And what about the impact on the storyteller's family? I
have a personal story to share that highlights how the mere act
of recording stories can bestow benefits on loved ones that are

impossible to understand at the time.

My father was in his late 60s when my daughter was very young; although we lived several hours away from him, he and she had a wonderful, silly relationship, sustained by my dad's child-like sense of humor and his penchant for sending her hilarious animatronic singing bears any chance he could. I knew my dad's full personality, his love of reading, his high regard for education and achievement, his ability to talk intelligently and at length on almost any subject (especially military history and Arthurian legend), and his ability to come up with a truly awful pun to inject into any conversation—and it occurred to me that perhaps my father would not live long enough for my daughter to come to know these aspects of his personality. I reached out to David to interview my dad and record stories from his life, thinking that this would be a gift to my daughter at some distant time down the road. After completing the editing, David sent me the recording, and I tucked it away, happy that it had been completed but not motivated to listen to it right away.

A year and a half later, I got the dreaded call: my father had suffered a sudden and fatal heart attack. It was unexpected and shocking; I was immediately thrown into the throes of grief. But one of the first thoughts I had after learning the news was of this recording that I had never listened to. Amid my grief, I felt what could almost be described as relief. In some way, I still had my dad—his voice, his stories. And three days after my dad's death, after dropping my daughter off at school, I sat in the car and listened to the interview. There was my dad—his terrible punny sense of humor, his laugh, his hopes and wishes for my daughter; and though I cried throughout, I realized that these were ultimately tears of gratitude. It struck me that, while I had embarked on this project for my daughter, it was ultimately a gift—and an absolutely priceless one—for me.

The stories people value most

Some of the stories that future generations enjoy the most are those that reach back multiple generations, explaining, for instance, how great-grandparents and grandparents lived, what they were like as individuals, their family traditions, and how they developed. While younger children can find it hard to visualize the world of decades ago, everyone can understand the concept of games, hobbies, and traditions. The stories do not need to contain overt messages but can speak for themselves. Especially meaningful is when people are willing to share the experience of hardships and how they were overcome. What did pivotal historical moments, actually lived first-hand, feel like? What was the tragic—or perhaps mundane—fallout? And, finally, every family member is entranced by romance. It never fails to grab a child or grandchild's attention to learn how couples in older generations met and fell in love.

No matter the specifics that emerge, the pure act of capturing the stories and voices of the past is something for which families are tremendously grateful. As David recounted, "For families there's a sense that they will have these stories forever. I often hear from families after the storyteller passes away. They tell me how grateful they are that we did the project."

Getting started

All too often, children only begin to develop an interest in who their parents and grandparents really are as they enter adulthood, yet this is often just the moment when the older generation begins to pass away. "Transferring that knowledge of those stories from one generation to the next—just that simple act is incredibly powerful. It doesn't have to be a grand undertaking," said David. "It's like the beauty of literature—you can dissect it to get enjoyment, or not. Different people find different meaning in the stories, at different levels... The story itself is the message. It's such a dense bundle... it contains lots of information. You don't have to tie it up in a bow." These stories can span 150 years, he added. "That in itself is remarkable. We take that knowledge for granted. We don't see the value in it because we're too immersed in it. Does the fish know the water in which it swims?"

However you go about capturing your family's stories—whether through the StoryCorps app, hiring a professional like David, or just getting a video going on your phone—start today. The interview with my father lasted two hours. It will be a gift that I, my daughter, her children, and beyond will have for the rest of their lives.

Questions to get you started on sharing family stories

General questions:

1. Which family stories would it be a shame to lose to history?

    ....
    ....
    ....

2. Which family stories might future generations take comfort in knowing or draw inspiration from?

    ....
    ....
    ....

3. Which family stories would make future generations laugh or smile?

    ....
    ....
    ....

4.   Which family stories might help future generations answer the question "Who am I?"

....

....

....

SPECIFIC QUESTIONS:

1.   What's the source of your name? Does it have a special meaning?

....

....

....

2.   Who are you more like, your mother or your father?

....

....

3.   When were you born? Where did you live? What was happening in the world at that time?

....

....

....

4. What is your very first memory? Why do you think you remember it? What is your strongest memory from each stage of your life?

....

....

....

....

....

....

5. What was your home like when you were a child? Describe it.

....

....

....

....

6. What did you like to do as a child? What was your favorite game? What did you want to be when you grew up?

....

....

....

....

7.   What were your parents like? Your grandparents?
      What do you know about their personalities and
      history?

....

....

....

....

....

....

....

8.   Did your family live through any pivotal moments in
      history? What were they like?

....

....

....

....

9.   Tell me about some of your friends and why you
      were close.

....

....

....

10. What was school like for you? What did you love or hate about school?

....
....
....

11. Tell me about the first time you fell in love.

....
....
....
....
....

12. What was it like becoming a parent? What are some special memories you have about each of your children?

....
....
....
....
....
....

13.   What is one moment in your work life that stands
      out for you?

....

....

....

14.   What were some difficult times in your life—how
      did you get through them?

....

....

....

....

....

15.   What is your favorite holiday tradition and why?
      Did you make new traditions or honor old ones?
      Why?

....

....

....

....

....

Clarifying the meaning behind your estate plan

In addition to family stories that might otherwise be lost for-ever, another story that only you can tell is the true intent and meaning—the "why"—behind your estate plan. The loved ones you leave behind will yearn to hear this from you directly; no matter how well your papers have been executed technically, your inheritors will not be able to divine your reasoning from the legal-ese in your estate planning documents.

Bob Mauterstock, a professional family facilitator, has two tragic stories that prove our point. In one case, a gregarious, bear of a man with two sons had spent his lifetime building a paving business that became highly successful. His sons had spent many years working in the business together and had an understanding about the division of responsibilities that worked well for them both.

In his will, the father, out of a quest for simplicity, left the ownership of the business to his older son, with the understand-ing and expectation that the older son would share the profits with the younger son in the form of compensation and other perks. But he never explained this rationale to his sons. As a con-sequence, the brothers got into an enormous argument; instead of being able to understand their father's thinking, they directed their anger and frustration toward each other. The older brother took control of the business, the younger cut off all communi-cation, and the two, despite having gotten along well all of their lives up until this point, never spoke to each other again.

In another case, two parents decided to leave their large wa-terfront home and accompanying acreage to one child and all of their significant stock funds to another. No one could have predicted that the property values would escalate while the stock values would plummet. Because the family had not talked about this decision before it was made and the parents did not explain their reasoning, the children's relationship became so strained that they broke off all contact.

"You have to be courageous," Mauterstock said. "It's not very easy to talk about these things. It's a lot easier in the moment to do nothing. But do you want to leave your family in that position, if you don't know what's going to happen when you're gone? The most important gift you can give your children is not anything tangible, it's the gift of communication. It's more valuable than any other gift you can give them."

Elizabeth Arnold decided to focus her career on helping people explain the motivations behind their wills, after hearing about the experience of a friend whose mother, Janet, had recently passed away. Janet had been stricken with cancer and was finally succumbing to the disease after a nine year battle. She had written her will, concentrating on how to divide up her assets among her three children. Then she overheard her two daughters making funeral plans; they had decided to ask people to donate to a breast-cancer research institute to honor their mother, in lieu of flowers. But this was not what Janet wanted. She preferred to focus on the passion that had driven her life—not the cause that would end it—and asked that donations be made instead to the local elementary school's library, where she had volunteered for many years. One daughter said, "As part of her will, I never even considered asking my mom about the values and legacy she wanted to pass on. In many ways, I thought it went without saying."[55]

They ended up raising thousands of dollars for the library, and a reading room was dedicated to their mother's memory. Each time they think of this legacy, they feel a surge of joy, knowing that they were able to honor what their mother cared about. This was such a formative experience that Elizabeth Arnold dedicated her career to helping others avoid this kind of potential confusion.

Why aren't legal documents enough?

Estate plans today are thick legal documents in which the majority of the document consists of standard legal and tax language required by law. You have to pick through them in incredible detail to discern anything that is uniquely representative of a person's wishes—and even then it is typically described in highly legal language, devoid of personality. This causes two problems.

First, estate documents are not where your children will be able to divine the meaning behind your wishes. When it is time for the proverbial "reading of the will" (which doesn't happen anymore because wills, or the revocable and other trust structures that have replaced them, are so complex), the reality of how much money goes where will convey none of the "whys" that children desperately want to know. Imagine how children feel when all they have to understand what Mom and Dad were thinking is 70-100 pages of legal language.

Second, sometimes the documents are so complicated and the reality of how the language will play out is so difficult to comprehend that it is hard even for the people to whom the wills belong to know whether they were written in a way that is consistent with their values and their hopes for their children. When we help our clients analyze the meaning behind their legal documents, we have to prepare multiple exhibits for them in an effort to tease out whether the actual meaning behind their documents is consistent with their wishes.

How to begin

In reality, explaining your reasoning to your inheritors is the last step in the process. The first step is ensuring that the way your estate plan works actually matches your values. To begin, think hard about your goals for your estate plan—not the nuts and bolts of where your money will go and how, but the larger, deeper goal of how you hope your plan will impact (or not impact) your children, their relationships with one another, and their memories of you.

Next, study your current plan to make sure that it actually carries out your wishes and is consistent with these goals. This takes a bit of looking into the future, thinking through possible scenarios, and imagining what impact these various scenarios will have on your children and their memories of you. You might need someone to help translate the legalese into numbers and pictures so that you can comprehend the story that they tell and make sure it plays out the way you hope.

Use the questions we've outlined in the following box as a guide for your thoughts. By the time you're done, you should be able to answer all of these questions, and you should make sure that the answers are consistent with what you hope and expect for your children and the way you hope they will remember you.

This is a process of serious self-reflection and one that you may need the help of an advisor to do thoroughly. But, again, think of this as a gift: how much time or money, or both, would you devote to avoiding sowing a conflict among your children that might destroy or impair their relationships with one another for the rest of their lives?

The stakes truly are that high—and the power is in your hands to do something to avoid this tragic outcome.

Questions to ask yourself to help you contemplate and convey the meaning behind your estate plan

General questions:

1. What are our goals for our children? How would we define a job well done as parents? Is our estate plan— and the way it will impact our children's lives—consistent with these goals?

    ....
    ....
    ....
    ....
    ....

2. What lessons and values have we tried to teach our children, and is our estate plan consistent with those?

    ....
    ....
    ....

3.   If our children or other heirs used our estate planning decisions to gauge our level of trust in them and our expectations of their abilities (especially relative to one another), what might they conclude? Are we happy with that?

....

....

....

4.   How would we feel if we were in our children's shoes and this were how our own parents' plans had read? Is there anything we'd want changed? Why?

....

....

....

5.   What do we hope our children or other heirs will feel about our estate plan once it becomes known to them? Would they feel that way now if they knew our plans? If not, why not?

....

....

....

....

SPECIFIC QUESTIONS:

1. Are we happy with the amount of money each of our children or other heirs is getting? And when they get it? And how?

   ....

   ....

   ....

   ....

   ....

   ....

   ....

   ....

2. If money is going to our children or other heirs in trust, are we happy with how the trust rules impact how they will be able to interact with the money? Will they work with a trustee for their whole lives? If so, are we happy with how this trustee will be selected and/or replaced?

   ....

   ....

   ....

   ....

3. If we have a family vacation home that we hope our children will continue to make happy memories in for several generations, is there money set aside to keep it in good condition? Are there provisions in place to help our children work out disagreements about who will spend time there and when? What happens if something goes wrong—if the property becomes unusable, the money runs out, or there is discord in the family? Are we happy with what our documents say about what will happen then?

....

....

....

....

....

Communicating your wishes

Once your own thinking is clear, the next critical step is to communicate these thoughts to your children. The goal is to eliminate uncertainty and stave off conflict by providing all of your heirs with transparent, consistent information about your wishes. They might not all agree with what you have done, but at least they will not have to fight about your intent.

Often I see people resist even contemplating this topic, much less communicating their thoughts to their children (either in person or in writing for later reading) because they worry that conflict might arise as a result of their choices or that their wishes might disappoint their children. But avoiding the topic now will not guarantee that future conflict is averted—in fact, the only thing it guarantees is that this conflict won't be addressed until you are no longer there to help resolve it (when you are actually the person in the best position to do so!).

So what options do you have for communication? If your children are old enough, gather them together and tell them personally. If they are too young, write your thoughts in a letter or record a video discussing why you made the decisions that you did and what your hopes are. It doesn't have to be a long conversation. Sometimes the simplest sentiments may have the longest-reaching benefits.

Recently I recorded an interview with clients of mine at their serene lakeside family retreat. During our two-hour interview, which touched on the couple's wishes and hopes for their children, the conversation turned to the beautiful home we were sitting in. The couple, without missing a beat, said that while this was a special property and they were very glad to have built it for the family, what was really most important about the house was that it facilitated their children's having good relationships and sharing their lives with one another. They said that if this ever ceased to be possible with this particular home, the children should recreate that somewhere else. Imagine how powerful that sentiment might be in the future, if conversations about how to keep and maintain the home began to sow discord in their family! What a difference that brief comment, which is reflected nowhere in their extensive estate planning documents, might make in the lives of their family members, perhaps for generations to come.

Pulling it all together: Creating your ethical will

So how do you do this in reality? You may have thoughts about family stories and the meaning behind your estate plan swirling around, eager to come out. Is there an effective format for communicating all of this—and more—in one fell swoop? In fact there is: it's called an ethical will. The historical concept of an ethical will traces back to Biblical times, and examples of ethical wills are evident in everything from Genesis—Jacob's dying words to his sons—to medieval fathers' dictums for their children that have survived (and seem relevant) to this day.

But in our modern era, the ethical will has evolved to mean a form of communication—a document, letter, or video—in which you convey all that you wouldn't want to go unsaid to those you will leave behind. It can contain the elements we've already talked about—family stories and the "why" behind your estate plan—but it can also include thoughts that represent the "you" you hope to leave with others when you are gone: messages of love, pride, or gratitude for loved ones, or values that you hold dear and hope will inspire future generations. In the words of Susan Turnbull, an ethical-will specialist who helps individuals and couples create their ethical wills through her company Personal Legacy Advisors, "An ethical will focuses on the inside aspects—your values, your intentions, your emotions. Wills are about what you want your loved ones to have. This is about what you want them to know."

The process of creating an ethical will prompts a level of self-reflection and introspection that people can find daunting initially but ultimately very rewarding. You are, in effect, contemplating your deepest, most closely held beliefs, values, and hard-won life lessons and your love, hopes, and dreams for others, and then distilling the essence of those reflections into a message for your loved ones, to be communicated either now or in the event that you never get a chance to say these things yourself.

To those reluctant to embark down this path, it's worth considering that the reflective process required to create an ethical will mirrors almost exactly the central developmental task that Erik Erikson identified with the last, "maturity" period of life, which happens between age 65 and death. Erikson posits that the central question in this last, "Wisdom" stage of life is this: Is it okay to have been me?

To answer this question, individuals reflect upon their past accomplishments, actions, and impact on others, and are ultimately able to come to an integrated, positive view of self if they conclude from this process that their life has been worthwhile. Andrew Weil, in his book *Healthy Aging*, picks up on this concept with his assertion that, "Certainly, an ethical will can be a wonderful gift to leave to your family at the end of your life, but I think its main importance is what it can give you in the midst of life."[56]

Susan shared the story of a couple she worked with who wanted to write an ethical will explaining to their children the values that drove their estate planning decisions. What started as an effort to set out their thinking for their children became an introspective exercise, in which the couple ultimately came to the conclusion that they needed to find a clearer focus for their own philanthropy. When Susan followed up with the couple to ask about the impact of this process on the family, they relayed that while their children appreciated having a permanent record of their parents' values and beliefs, the biggest impact of the exercise had been on their own thinking—it had forced a conversation between the two of them that ultimately led to a much stronger conviction in their own philanthropic efforts. This sense that the process—of confirming what's important to you and seeing an arc to your life—is its own reward is nearly universal among her clients, Susan says. They tell her, "I am so glad I did this—that I forced myself to make the effort."

Beyond the reward of self-reflection, completing an ethical will provides enormous peace of mind that you will never be caught unawares, that if the unthinkable happens, you won't be deprived of the chance to relay the last messages you would have imparted to loved ones. In the aftermath of September 11, 2001, National Public Radio's Toviah Smith filed a story about how the tragedy was prompting people to write their own ethical wills.[57] One woman she interviewed, Paula Feinman from Newton, Massachusetts, talked about being haunted by the story of a mother calling on her cell-phone from within one of the towers, desperate to reach her child in daycare. "If, God forbid," Paula thought, "the worst happens and I can't communicate with my child, how can I be the one who gives them the message that I want them to hear after I'm dead?" Her solution was to write a message to both of her daughters telling them how much she loved them and passing on the core nuggets of life wisdom that she hoped would guide them well on their paths in life.

Even when tragedy doesn't intervene and life is allowed to run its course, an ethical will can be useful when the dynamics of the parent-child relationship mean that these messages might never be spoken out loud. Susan often finds that her clients share in writing what they wouldn't verbally. One grandfather told her, "I wouldn't sit down with my boys and tell them this. I'm not comfortable talking about myself." But he wanted to be genuinely understood by his sons and grandchildren, and a written ethical will provided him with the means to do that.

And what about the benefits to the family? As with shared stories, families are almost universally grateful when a parent or grandparent has gone to the effort to create an ethical will. This is partly because the historical "father knows best" type of ethical will has largely given way to the more modern, egalitarian format of "I want you to know what I think, not because you should be or act a certain way but because it's important to me that you know." Children appreciate having the essence of their parents or grandparents—their core beliefs, values, and hopes for loved ones—captured and preserved against any changes to come.

This can be especially meaningful to a family in the case of dementia or mental decline. Susan Turnbull relayed the story of several sisters who asked her to help their parents craft an ethical will as a gift to their children and grandchildren. Their aim was to capture their parents and make them more real for their children down the road, and they thought that having an objective third person doing the questioning would make it easier for their parents to engage (they were right—this is often the case). Over the course of several sessions, the parents' words spilled out—family stories, reflections, beliefs, and hopes and feelings for their grandchildren, all captured in a document that could be read for many generations to come. Several years later, Susan learned from one of the sisters that their father had developed dementia. They were so grateful that they had done the project when they had, as it wouldn't have been possible now.

So how to get started? It helps to start small, and in order of highest priority. What are the few thoughts or sentences you would most want to convey to your loved ones if tragedy strikes and you aren't able to have that last conversation? Then expand to the life lessons you hold dear and would most want to convey. When Susan finds people stuck, feeling like they aren't old enough or wise enough to begin this process, she suggests a simple exercise: list the "Ten Things I Know to Be True." Spending a half-hour or an hour jotting down the lessons that spring to mind tends to get the juices flowing—and often carries people 80% of the way toward a final document.

Consider hiring a professional to help (see the resources section at the end of this chapter), or use the questions in the box below to get started on your own. And understand that whatever you say now can change. It's better to get started today than to wait for the perfect moment. Think of the recipients of lifetime achievement awards: there's probably no year when they feel sufficiently old to deserve it, but they'd rather win it than not!

Questions to help you get started on your ethical will

1.   What would I say to my children or loved ones in my
      last moments? What would I not want to leave unsaid?

....

....

....

....

....

2. What are the values that have played a meaningful role in my life?

....

....

....

....

3. How would I like to be thought of after I'm gone? What would I like my loved ones to celebrate about my life?

....

....

....

....

....

4. What would I like future generations that I may never have the chance to meet to know about me?

....

....

....

....

....

5.   What are my greatest hopes and wishes for my loved
      ones? What message could I give them to provide
      comfort or inspiration in their lives?

....

....

....

....

....

6.   In what ways do I want to have an enduring positive
      impact on the people I will leave behind?

....

....

....

....

....

The beauty of leaving an "organic" legacy

In his book *How to Say It to Seniors*, author David Solie identifies three types of legacy that people can leave behind: the default legacy, the political legacy, and the organic legacy. The default legacy is when there has been no plan—a passive process that can therefore leave an inaccurate portrait of a life lived. The political legacy is more technical than heartfelt, more process-driven than authentic—it is about tangibles such as money and property. Finally, there is the organic legacy, which is "predicated on gathering appropriate data—memories, thoughts, facts, emotions. It is a time-consuming, exhaustive, ultimately redemptive process that contextualizes everything that may have been misinterpreted, misunderstood, or unrepaired in a person's life. How well we facilitate this stage of the person's development has a direct impact on how...the person will be remembered, and how well that person's life will impact future generations."[58]

In other words, yes, it's work, but it's worth it. Let this be a project that you begin today. Of all the things you can do in later life that will positively and meaningfully impact generations to come, this one is high on the list.

Resources for recording family stories and histories

VIDEO / FILM

Pam Pacelli Cooper and Rob Cooper, Verissima Productions (verissima.com/)—Cambridge, MA

Andy Greenspan, Docyoumentary (docyoumentary.com/)—Palm Beach Gardens, FL

Bob Jordan, Jordan & Jordan Communications, Inc. (www.videofamilybiographies.com/)—Chicago, IL

Daniella Topol, LIVES: Your Story on Film (livesfilms.com/)—New York City

Iris Wagner, Memoirs Productions (memoirsproductions.com/)—Montreal, Canada

ORAL HISTORIES AND/OR WRITTEN MEMOIRS

David O'Neil, Story Trust (www.storytrust.com/)—Newton, MA

StoryCorps app (storycorps.org/)

21/64 Toolkits, particularly *What Am I Inheriting?* and *The Family Diagram* (2164.net/store)

Resources for creating your ethical will

WORKBOOKS / TOOLS

The Wealth of Your Life: A Step-by-Step Guide for Creating Your Ethical Will by Susan Turnbull
(www.personallegacyadvisors.com/)

Stanford Medicine Life Review Letter Project
(med.stanford.edu/letter/friendsandfamily.html)

21/64 Toolkits, particularly *Picture Your Legacy* and *Motivational Values Cards* (2164.net/store)

BOOKS

Creating the Good Will: The Most Comprehensive Guide to Both the Financial and Emotional Sides of Passing on Your Legacy by Elizabeth Arnold

Ethical Wills: Putting Your Values on Paper (2nd ed.), by Barry K. Baines, M.D., and the tools on his website
(celebrationsoflife.net/)

Your Legacy Matters: a Multi-generational Guide for Writing Your Ethical Will by Rachael Freed

Having the Last Say: Capturing Your Legacy in One Small Story by Alan Gelb

The LastingMatters Organizer: Where loved ones find what matters most by Barbara Bates Sedoric
(www.lastingmatters.com/)

CHAPTER SEVEN
CHANGING BODIES AND MINDS

....

Developing a Plan for Dealing with Life's Twists and Turns

In writing this book, we spoke with older people who have found ways to live a fulfilling later life and asked them how they made this happen. We spoke with many who shared insights about how to be energetic, engaged, hopeful, and passionate as they enter and make their way through old age. Our interviewees work hard to keep their bodies and minds intact, and it is paying off for them: they feel great; they are youthful; they're both realistic and optimistic; and they're willing to work hard to stay in the game.

Yet, inexorably, people's bodies and minds weaken. While there is much that we can do to try to stay healthy and capable, it's likely that for most of us there will come a time when we'll experience some decline in our capacities—physical or mental— and will need a little help. This is a frightening thought, and as a result it's not a thought we like to dwell on. It stirs up all sorts of uncomfortable unknowns: How might this happen? What will it be like? Will I be able to manage and accept the changes that occur?

As with most fears, the key to conquering this one is to face it head on, plan ahead, and focus on what you can control—which turns out to be a lot. You can choose where you will want to live; you can think ahead now about what supports will best allow you to create a fulfilling life for yourself, despite declines in physical or mental ability; and you can plan for whom you would like to have on tap to provide any care that you need.

Most importantly, you can discuss your plans with your family so they have clarity about your wishes and will not be forced to make impossible decisions in times of stress, perhaps in conflict with you. Our interviewee Cynthia eloquently expressed the anxiety most children feel when the plans for their aging parents remain unclear. Although her vibrant, 82-year-old mother, Deirdre, "was always the energy in my parents' marriage, making the plans for the family," she has not communicated her plans to her daughter for how she sees the remainder of her life unfolding. Deirdre is still engaged and independent, and Cynthia doesn't know how to bring it up.

"Do not go gently into the night—that's my mother!" Cynthia said. "I do think she's having a hard time with the idea of not being here." And yet Cynthia wishes she knew more about what her mother wants and how she would like things to progress if she can no longer live independently. "What I would really like to see are things like, when would you determine that you can't live on your own anymore? Would she want to have somebody live in with her—would you want to move in with me?" ("Please God, no!" Cynthia added, laughing heartily.) "Would she want to go to a senior residence? When would that be? Would you want to be at home, being basically unconscious? Those are big questions! Those are things I'd love to have answered." Even though they are close, Cynthia and Deirdre have not yet found a way to broach this uncomfortable subject. Imagine the relief Cynthia would feel if Deirdre one day took the first step and announced proactively that she would like to discuss her options.

Indeed, the first step in bridging this communication divide is to do the work in your own mind to clarify your wishes for how you would like this chapter of your life to unfold. Where will you want to live? What supports will you need if and when you can no longer manage the details or logistics of an independent life perfectly well on your own? How would you like your loved ones to act if you begin to experience cognitive impairment? These are not simple questions, and answering them takes an understanding not only of the options available to you but also an imagining of the types of situations you might find yourself in. It's a taxing mental exercise and not one that would rank high on anyone's list of most enjoyable. But these are decisions that you will want to make yourself—as opposed to having someone else make for you.

It's only when your answers to these questions are clear in your own mind that you can take the next step, which is communicating your thoughts to your loved ones. In our interviews, we heard a number of moving stories from grown children whose parents had given them this gift of clarity around their wishes for this phase of life. The peace of mind these individuals feel is palpable and lasting. That is the goal of this chapter: to show you that this can be done well, and to help you see how. In the process, we will highlight the issues you need to think about so that you too can be in a position to impart this sense of gratitude and peace to your loved ones.

Home is where the heart is

We'll start with where you will want to live, as that is typically the issue that is most emotionally fraught. In our national lore, home is more than a place to live—it is a metaphor for success, family, self-reliance, and independence. As a result—and also partially as a result of inertia, which shouldn't be underestimated as a powerful force as we age—the natural inclination for most people, when asked where they would like to spend their older years, is "at home."

However, since we're planning ahead and going deep into the heart of the types of physical and mental limitations that are most common in our later years, we need to look at what home really means as we age, particularly in the context of what types of living arrangements will best allow us to live out Section One's four characteristics of vibrant aging. In many ways, it comes down to framing the right question. Rather than asking, "Where will I live when I'm older?" we should ask, "What environment will best allow me to cultivate the four factors as I age?" Framing the problem this way allows us to see the issue fully and expose the thorny realities that need to be paid attention to if we are thinking ahead.

One of the reasons that the issue of where to live is so challenging is that the nature of home shifts as people age and their capacities decline. If you're leading a healthy and vibrant older life, home is a home base—it is the place from which you reach out to lead a connected, engaged, purposeful life. You enjoy cooking for and hosting your friends, you remain current and involved because you can easily drive or walk to your favorite restaurants, theaters, or museums, and the task of managing the house is not so arduous that you don't have time left in the day for the projects and work that give you meaning. In short, home is the place from which you are best able to cultivate the four factors. You are in charge and autonomous, authoring your own life.

But a funny thing starts to happen as we age, around this axis of autonomy. There can come a point when diminishing capacities mean that it's no longer possible to reach out from home to a connected, full, driven existence. When cooking and gardening are more of a burden than a joy, when the 10 minute walk downtown is inconveniently long on a bad knee, or the five minute drive to the evening show is no longer possible now that you no longer drive at night, the life that you are able to reach from home narrows considerably. You no longer author your existence with the same degree of freedom because either the tasks you must do have grown too burdensome or the things you want to do have become out of reach. In fact, it can start to feel as if the home owns you. Our interviewees shared with us many stories of parents who had gone through this type of transition, who slowly, over a period of years, found that home was no longer the base around which a full life revolved but rather a confining, burdensome albatross that in many ways institutionalized a lonely and constrained existence.

Even familiarity—another primary reason people choose to remain at home—begins to morph. When you are vibrantly older, the familiarity of the family home feels welcoming and reassuring: the kitchen where you have cooked your favorite meals, the garden with the plants you've tended for years, the community and neighborhood filled with places and people you enjoy. But when declining capacities make it harder to engage in these activities that used to be enjoyable, familiarity can morph into nostalgia or a sense of loss—everything you encounter on a daily basis in these familiar settings is a reminder of what you can no longer do.

This is not to say that it is impossible to enjoy a meaningful, connected later life while remaining at home. It's just that it may not be possible without some significant planning and supplementing. Ask yourself: Who will do the cooking if you are no longer able to yourself? How will you get to the places you want to go if you can't drive? How will you see friends if it's too much trouble to host a get-together and if your friends, perhaps dealing with their own limitations, have trouble getting to you? What will you do for intellectual stimulation if it's harder to visit town or attend classes?

There are answers to all of these questions, and most of them involve developing or tapping into a support network that you don't currently need. Some communities have attempted to tackle these issues through volunteer groups—either elders helping one another or senior centers that provide outreach services. And of course there are aides and caregivers who can be hired. But the point is that, if you are intent on remaining in your home, there will likely be some shift that will occur from the independent life you lead now to one in which you will need to lean on various supports. Begin now to plan for how you will manage this shift and get the support you need—not just to do tasks that you are no longer able or willing to do, but also, more importantly, to ensure that you continue to remain steeped and engaged in life in the way you were when you had the energy and inclination to reach out into the world. This last piece is the hardest to supplement and is the piece that degraded the most in the stories our interviewees shared of parents whose lives got smaller and narrower as they aged in place.

Of course, another possible way to supplement capabilities is to move to a community ready-built to address all of these needs. The senior-living market is quite robust already and will only continue to grow in the coming years as demographics demand. Many of the high-end senior-living places are designed around maximizing quality of life in later years, allowing you to cultivate the capabilities that you have remaining and providing support for areas where you have difficulty. The aim seems to be reduce reminders of what you can no longer do (chores—no problem, there's housekeeping; driving at night—no problem, there's no need, since activities, concerts, lectures, movies, etc. are brought to you) while focusing on what you can—making and managing friendships, participating in book clubs, discussion groups, art classes, cooking workshops, exercise classes, etc.

In fact, it's hard to look at the weekly calendar of one of these communities and think of an environment more optimally designed to support the four factors. It's easy to gather with friends because they live right down the hall and you can eat together every night in the common dining room. Continual learning opportunities are available daily in the form of lectures, classes, trips, and concerts. The mixture of freedom in choice of activities with support for areas of life that have become burdensome promotes a sense of competence and agency, and the time saved by eliminating activities that are no longer fulfilling can be redirected to new, purposeful projects.

And this is not just true on paper. If you know a relative in one of these communities, you have probably seen the culture that this type of community can create: actively engaged, vibrant older people trying new activities, making new friends, even feeling newly encouraged about aging itself as they find themselves surrounded by individuals who may be much older but seem to still be living full, connected, vibrant, and purposeful lives. Remember the story of Donald's mother from Chapter Two and how her move to a senior community at age 85 gave her a new lease on life? Her story is both deeply moving and not that unusual. These communities are full of people who have similar stories, whose move provided them with a way to drastically improve the quality of their lives, often in ways they couldn't have envisioned before the transition.

Of course, all of the communities that make up the constellation of living arrangements that are marketed to seniors are not the same, and if you are seriously contemplating a move to one of these communities, you have to do your research. There are full-service, continuing-care retirement communities (CCRCs), where a sizeable buy-in virtually guarantees that you will have a place there for the rest of your days; there are full-service, senior rental communities that rival luxury New York City apartment buildings for amenities (movie theaters, swimming pools, etc.); and there is everything in between, both in terms of economic models and amenities.

The whole process is uncannily reminiscent of choosing a college, and like the college process, it's worth taking a tour. What does the place really feel like? Do you think you could feel at home there? Could these people be your new best friends? Do you like the activities that are on the roster and can you actually picture yourself going to any of them? And what about the cultural norms—how the dining hall works, how social gatherings materialize, how many activities you are encouraged to go to versus what is free time? If that all checks out, what about the community and the neighborhood? Is there anywhere nearby that you would be excited to walk to? Is it located in a place where you will still feel you're part of life and connected to the world? Will you have a chance on a regular basis to see anyone outside your age group? If you hope your children will visit, is it in a location convenient to them?

Finally, just like college, there is the last question—will you get in? It's common for the most desirable places to have waiting lists of several months to several years, and, particularly for the continuing-care communities, once you come up in the queue, there are cognitive assessments, community interviews, and financial questionnaires, all designed to determine whether you will be a good fit for the community and whether you can afford it. Some of these communities will admit you only if you do sufficiently well on the cognitive assessments to qualify to live independently for several years—which is why it can be important not to wait too long to make this transition, if you think you may eventually want to go down this route.

What really matters is that you want a place that will be focused on helping you flourish in your later years and that will maximize your capacity to continue doing what you are able to do at the outer bounds of your capacities. As Atul Gawande describes in his book *Being Mortal*, you want a place that will actually assist you with living,[59] which is not possible if the focus of the caregivers is on completing tasks (getting all the residents dressed) rather than on helping people flourish (having the patience to allow residents to work hard to dress themselves if they are capable, even if it takes longer).

These and other examples are emblematic of a central tension that Gawande observes: the traditional eldercare model often strikes a dissatisfactory balance between the "safety" that is wanted for the residents by their families (and implemented by the facility's often well-meaning but highly regulated staff) and the "autonomy" that residents typically want for themselves—the right to risk falling, for instance, if it means being able to walk to the library rather than ride in a wheelchair, or the right to miss breakfast if it means being able to wake at a time of their own choosing. As a result of the historical, and still common, institutional priority on safety, the annals of eldercare are sadly filled with stories of individuals whose lives were just as, if not more, confined and restrained in care settings.

This model is changing, however. Gawande sees hope in the growing number of communities that are structured differently, where priority is placed not only on safety but, more broadly, on helping residents to lead worthwhile lives. A number of pioneers are spearheading this movement. One, Richard Landry, in his book *Live Long, Die Short*, talks about the culture that he and his colleagues intentionally set out to cultivate: "We spent the next three years developing tools and resources to help a community evolve its culture from one where comfort and security were the defining characteristics to one where growth was the currency, from a culture that provided what a zoo does for its residents to one that provided what a university does for its students: a culture where physical, intellectual, social, and spiritual growth is expected, nurtured, and facilitated. This brought us into new territory, where *every* staff member in the community had a role in culture; where the environment moved from a cruise ship–entertainment approach to one of growth; from a medical, paternalistic, 'We'll help you when you get sick' model, to an approach of 'Tell us how we can help you be all you can be.'"[60]

In your research, keep this dichotomy in mind. The new setting Landry describes is the kind of culture you want to look for, and you want the ethos of growth to be embedded in the place, from the chief executive down to every caregiver you meet. You can interview residents on this point, and you can ask what life is really like in the community day to day—not just when you are still able to live independently, but also as capacities decline and you require more help.

Use your resources wisely

As you can see, there is a lot of to do to be prepared for this next phase of life. Think of the resources you can marshal and use them to your advantage. One resource is time, and, if you're lucky, time is on your side and you can begin planning now. Think proactively about what setting will give you the best chance at flourishing at each stage of your later life, and understand that the answer may shift over time. It can be hard to imagine needing support or moving out of your home in your vibrant and capable older years, but if you wait until a change is obviously needed, it's often too late—if you're staying at home, it can be too late to identify and cultivate an optimal support network; and if you choose to move, it can be too late not only to identify the place you would most like to go to (or even to qualify for it) but also to be sufficiently energetic and capable to acclimate to the new environment and make new friends when you get there. Many who successfully make a move like this and enjoy their new community remark that they wish they had moved earlier. Moving earlier also allows you to take advantage of all of the activities and socialization these places offer, which can keep your mind engaged and challenged more effectively than leading a confined, narrow, lonely existence.

The other resource is, of course, financial means. This is an area where having wealth is a distinct advantage. If you have means, you are in an ideal position either to hire the resources you need to supplement a later life in your home or to identify a place where you would enjoy living and use your means to secure a spot. Don't squander this opportunity by not doing your home-work—think deeply about your options and choose the place or situation you would enjoy the most. Given that this decision will greatly impact not only your own quality of life as you age, but also your loved ones' peace of mind, it ranks high among the list of worthwhile uses of your time and money.

The benefits of being proactive

Whatever you decide, make it something *you* decide. With-out your proactive thought and planning, this is often a decision that is made on the fly, hopefully by a loving relative but still in a time of crisis, stress, and limited options. You don't want to leave it to your children to flail as they attempt to identify and address your increasing inability to manage life and care for yourself in a setting that is no longer appropriate.

In Chapter One we heard the story of my colleague Leah's grandfather, Bud, who voluntarily sat for driving tests as he got older after being inspired to deal proactively with his own aging by the difficult experience he and his wife had had caring for her parents. Another proactive step that Bud and his wife Grace took was deciding to sell their home and move to a continuing-care community long before a crisis dictated that choice. Looking around at their large three-story home, they anticipated that a day would come when they would no longer be able to manage it independently. Because they planned ahead and made the move long before it was necessary, they felt young when they moved into their independent cottage in the new community and invested in developing a host of new friendships. As time went on, they downsized from their independent cottage to an independent apartment and then eventually to an assisted-living arrangement, when, in their 90s, they needed additional care. By taking these steps on their own, before they needed to, Bud and Grace gave their family members a palpable gift.

Indeed, the impact on your children of your plans—whether voiced or unvoiced, carried out or simply typed up and waiting in a drawer—shouldn't be underestimated. Although it's certainly mental work to think through your options and decide which ones you prefer, it's not enough. The next step is to bring your children into the discussion, not only to inform them of your plans but, more importantly, to test your assumptions and see if they agree with your thinking. For instance, if a critical factor in your choice of living arrangement is that it is close to one of your children, it's important to talk with this child about how much time he or she will have to visit. Or, if you have decided that you can remain in your home as long as you hire an aide, do your children agree that this arrangement will work? Does this address any concerns they have about your well-being, or would additional support be helpful? And, most important of all, are your children in agreement? If three of your four children assume the fourth will handle these conversations and any planning that needs to be done, does the fourth agree?

Involving your children and getting everyone on the same page becomes important because the transition from vibrant and capable older living to a situation where some degree of help is necessary is rarely neat and orderly. Often there are steps forward and back, good days and bad, and disparate opinions on how capable a parent is of living on his or her own. You want to have as many of these discussions as possible before crises arise, so that siblings don't have to invent the language of how to discuss a situation while it's unfolding.

Our interviewee Debbie shared with us a story that illustrated how important it can be for siblings to be in the know and in agreement about their parents' preferred plans before a crisis erupts. Debbie was spending most of her time in Arizona with her husband, Raymond, when her mother, Faith—still living in New Jersey, and living alone since her husband died—began showing signs of dementia. Faith would sit by herself in her living room all day long, watching television. She became confused by instructions on how to boil noodles. Her sense of time became warped: at age 91, she signed up for a 10-year subscription to *People* magazine. And then a crisis occurred. Debbie got a frantic call one night from one of the neighbors: there was smoke billowing out of the windows, and fire trucks were parked outside Faith's house. She had left the oven on and burned her dinner while she sat, unaware, watching *Judge Judy* on TV.

Because Debbie and her siblings had talked with their mother at length about her wishes for where she wanted to live as she got older, they knew that her strong preference was to remain in her home and had already agreed on a plan that would make this possible. As a result, rather than having to begin this difficult discussion in the middle of a crisis, they were able to start putting the plan into place immediately: Debbie's sister lived nearby and was able to arrange her schedule so that, between her efforts and a local day program, they could provide Faith with the support she needed to remain in her home for the next several years until her death. "It was very gratifying and validating that we were able to do these things for her," Debbie said. "The more you can communicate and understand what the stages are and can have dialogue, the better… Fear and not talking is the problem."

Getting started

So, hopefully you feel prepared now to begin this process in your own family—to think deeply about which living arrangement will be best for you and then to communicate your thinking to your children and hear their reactions. Whatever choices you make, our interviewees agreed that it is critical to:

- Cultivate an attitude that is geared toward helping you live a contented later life. (i.e. Don't be so fearful or negative that you cannot be happy no matter what you choose.)

- Avoid operating on assumptions: do research, visit communities, and gather stories from people who have lived through similar transitions. Consider hiring a consultant to help you with this process. There are specialists in this area who know the communities inside and out and can help you assess which ones best fit your needs and preferences.

- Ask yourself hard questions: Why am I intent on this or that path? What am I most afraid of?

- Talk about options early and frequently, with your spouse and also with your children. Allow loved ones to help you: listen and weigh options, even (particularly!) when there is disagreement.

- Have clarity around finances, and—wherever you wish to live later—be sure to use funds to buy the best contingency plans and support you can afford (consultants, move managers, concierge healthcare, entrance to the continuing-care community of your choice, in-home care, etc.).

- Be willing to reassess your ideas periodically, taking into account changed circumstances or desires.

- Think not only about your own wishes but also about the impact those wishes will have on your children and on how they will remember this stage of your life and their time with you.

Questions to ask yourself to help you contemplate where you want to live later in life and communicate your preferences to your children

1.   What living environment will best allow me to cultivate the four factors of vibrant aging as I get older?

....

....

....

2. If I wish to remain in my home in my later years, what resources will I need to supplement what I am able to do for myself now? What support system will best allow me to continue to engage with the world?

....

....

3. If I'm interested in moving into a senior community, do I see myself being able to flourish there? Is the community organized to allow me to operate at the maximum of my capacities, whatever they may be at the time? Is this value embedded in the organization and at every level of staff?

....

....

4. Have I discussed my thoughts and preferences with my children? Are they in agreement with my plans? Do they have concerns? If so, how might I address these concerns as part of my planning process?

....

....

....

....

5.   If I'm happy living in my home now but envision
      making a change sometime in the future, how will I
      know when that time has arrived? What are the signs
      that will tell me it is time to make a change? Have I
      discussed these signs with my children, and do they
      agree that these should be the benchmarks? Are there
      any others they have in mind?

....

....

....

....

....

6.   When the time arrives to make a change, how would I
      like my children to act if I don't initiate the change on
      my own? What would I like them to do to make this
      change possible?

....

....

....

....

....

....

7. Do I expect any one or more of my children to take
    a primary role in helping me manage this process, if
    I need help? Do my children understand the roles I
    hope they will play, and are they willing to play them?
    Do they agree among themselves that these roles make
    sense?

....

....

....

....

....

Managing the specter of dementia

When asked what they most feared, our interviewees ad-
mitted that, more than anything, they were afraid of losing their
cognitive abilities. The fear our interviewees expressed is not un-
founded: according to the Alzheimer's Association, the risk of developing dementia doubles every five years starting at age of 65;
by age 85, the risk of having the disease is 50%.[61]

Among just some of the changes that dementia can bring
about are difficulty remembering recent conversations, names,
and events; an inability to manage routine aspects of life, such
as paying the bills or maintaining a house; apathy; depression;

disorientation; confusion; and poor judgment. These changes are typically not only greatly debilitating to the person suffering from the disease but also very taxing on family members, as they try to understand and diagnose their loved one's decline and intervene when possible or when the person will allow.

Dementia can also put an enormous strain on family harmony. It can be difficult for family members (not to mention advisors) to reach consensus on whether a person is truly suffering from cognitive impairment and to what degree. One sibling might look at Dad and think he is simply being forgetful, whereas another might view the constant forgetfulness as dangerous and indicative of a larger decline. The lack of agreement among the children (and possibly even the spouse) about what behaviors are concerning enough to warrant someone stepping in and forcing a change can create strife within the family and cause uncertainty and delay, which often compound the problem. No one can remember what the benchmarks were: How long was Mom like this? Was Dad always so short-tempered? Is the confusion he is exhibiting age-appropriate or alarming?

In addition, even if family members are able to reach consensus that something must be done, loved ones often experience a tremendous amount of guilt when forced to intervene, if they have never had the opportunity to discuss this possibility with their elders. Although a child may have no choice but to take control away from a parent who is cognitively impaired, it can still feel wrong; the natural order of life has been upset. It is especially hard for adult children when their parents actively resist. A typically trusting, easygoing parent may—fueled by the paranoia that is often a symptom of the disease—question family member's motives or accuse them of trying to steal money or benefit themselves. A child needing to step in can be made to feel like the bad guy, not only by the ailing parent but also by a sibling or other loved one if there is not sufficient agreement within the family about what types of behavioral changes necessitate a change.

Yet, despite being faced with the alarmingly high odds that a loved one in the family will develop dementia, most families do little planning for this eventuality, often because there is a sense of helplessness that nothing can be done. Or perhaps families think they have done what they can, because their estate documents are in order and they have named a Durable Power of Attorney or a successor trustee of a living trust. But these legal steps do little to address the long, slippery slope between active, healthy, later life functioning and the moment when all family members agree that an elder has diminished capacity. And it is in that long, slippery slope that most family strife and conflict occur.

We actually think there is much that can be done. What if you viewed the potential that you might develop dementia as one possible scenario you might encounter in life, one that can be planned for as you would any other? Think of the analogy of a house fire. The thought of your house burning down is frightening and tragic, but, rather than ignoring the problem and hoping for the best, you purchase homeowner's insurance. You don't fret over how terrible the eventuality would be if it occurred, but in the back of your mind you know that you have a plan and the means to address it. You can think of dementia in the same way— and when you do, all of a sudden this large, looming, frightening problem starts to look more matter-of-fact and manageable.

The key is to envision the decisions you might have to make in the future and make them now for your future self. This is the challenge of dementia, and where the analogy to the house fire ends. In most tragic situations that we encounter in life, we can count on our faculties and reasoning to get us through the crisis. With dementia, however, we have to marshal our faculties and our reasoning now. We have to imagine possible futures in which we are unable to plan or speak for ourselves and then do that planning and speaking now.

The bright side is that, with work, this can be done. It's quite possible to make decisions now that you may not be in a position to make later, and you can communicate your wishes now so that your family knows the game plan regardless of what the future holds. The simple act of walking through a dementia scenario and understanding what roles people will play and the triggers that will create these roles will eradicate much of the stress that family members feel when having to make decisions on the fly, often in times of crisis and racked with guilt over whether they are faithfully executing a parent's wishes. Coming to an agreement now, as a family and perhaps with advisors, will not erase guilt and discomfort entirely, but it will certainly mitigate them.

Speaking for your future self

Sarah Putnam, a journalist and videographer, has produced pieces that help people share stories and prepare for conversations about later life. She herself experienced first-hand the unparalleled gift of having a father who believed that part of his responsibility as a caretaker meant that he should prepare his family for all eventualities—not knowing that this would give his loved ones the chance to hear his voice and guiding principles even when he could no longer speak for himself.

An international banker, George was an old-fashioned, funny, generous-hearted man. By nature a planner, he bought a burial plot in his 40s; in his 50s, he convened the family with a lawyer to discuss his will, durable power of attorney, and a Do Not Resuscitate Order (DNR). "The lawyer made both my parents articulate how they got to that," Sarah said, "what they expected of me and what they hoped for, and what they didn't want and why." One point her father was adamant about was that he did not want any measures taken to keep him alive if he could no longer care for himself. Sarah was in her late 20s then, and taken by surprise: her father was healthy, and she hadn't even begun thinking about her parents' eventual demise.

After that, George began an annual tradition on New Year's Day of going through his later-life and end-of-life wishes with his family. "It became a family joke," Sarah told us. "He looked on it as a personal responsibility." She and her mother laughingly called it "the annual dirge." Her father would sit at his desk with a yellow legal pad and a pencil, writing down updates on such topics as "What to do if your mother and I go down in a plane crash." It included who to call first; where the family assets were; how to find the safety deposit box; a reminder about their burial plot; where he wanted his memorial service held; which hymns and prayers he wanted; and who his first, second, and third choices were to give eulogies ... among many other decisions.

"Dad had really thought this out—and he'd thought it out from multiple perspectives because that's who he was," Sarah said. "He thought about what made him most comfortable for his personal experience, but also about what made him the most comfortable in feeling that my mother was taken care of and would not be burdened, and that I would be taken care of and not burdened."

Too soon thereafter, in an unpredictable twist of fate, early-onset Alzheimer's disease robbed George of his ability to communicate. His wife cared for him at home as long as she could, until he moved into a facility for the last few years of his life. One day the family got a call that he had developed pneumonia: did they want to begin a course of antibiotics? "That's a really, really hard call for someone to deal with if you're not prepared for that," Sarah explained. Antibiotics are non-invasive, a simple first line of defense—and withholding them means almost certain death. "But my mother and I didn't have any anguish, we didn't have to hesitate... He had already made the decisions, and it was easy for us to honor his choices."

Not only did his preparations make those hard choices easier; they also allowed George to participate beyond the time when he was physically or mentally capable of doing so. "He'd laid the groundwork," Sarah said. "It really was a gift. And it was like he was part of the process, and that was a gift too... It allowed him some control right to the end. He was still taking care of his family."

She emphasized that leaving these kinds of conversations till later, when people are vulnerable, is not a good plan. "Talk about it from a position of strength, when you can be proactive, not reactive," she said.

What you can do now

In addition to making end-of-life decisions that might be impossible for you to make later (more on this in the next chapter), you can begin now to think through the nuances of a dementia scenario and plan for how you would want your loved ones to act in that event.

How can you get started on this process? First, take a deep breath, then plunge into the list of questions that we have detailed in the box at the end of this chapter. There are questions to think about with your spouse, your advisors, and your children. The goal is to think ahead—to put yourself mentally in a place where this is happening now—and envision how it will unfold and how you would want everyone to act. For instance, what types of mental changes do you think should be an indication to everyone that you need help and would like someone to step in? Imagine what a relief it would be to your children if you spelled this out now.

Once you have thought through the questions we list, take the next step and write a letter to your children or record a video expressing your wishes. Even if you have a conversation with your children in the here and now on the topic, there is nothing more valuable than an indelible record they can use as a reminder of your wishes when you may no longer be able to voice them yourself.

Aside from the clarity a record like this provides, the emotional benefit is significant. Children who might otherwise feel racked with guilt over having to step in and remove authority from a parent feel absolved when they see a record in their parent's voice asking them to do just that. Siblings who might otherwise have disagreed about what type of behavior is problematic can now all point to the same specific symptoms that their parents themselves articulated. And there is far less arguing over what steps the family should take and what care arrangements would be best when parents have said in their own words what arrangement they would prefer. This type of record is particularly valuable in situations where a child has to take action over a parent's objections. The child can refer to the record and remind themselves that "Mom or Dad, when they were healthy, would have wanted me to do exactly what I'm doing now."

The road ahead

At this point you may be feeling a bit overwhelmed or even dispirited, contemplating the challenging work we are recommending. Yet, while there is no silver lining in the diagnosis of dementia or Alzheimer's disease, we are convinced that careful planning can be not only an invaluable gift to one's family but also a truly rewarding experience for yourself along the way. After all, you can be proud of the courageous and thoughtful work you are undertaking for your family and loved ones, and you can help ensure that your preferences for how you would want to live will be honored.

"Aging is not a disease," writes Sherwin Nuland, M.D., in *The Art of Aging*. "It is the condition upon which we have been given life."[62] And it is within our power to do far more than simply accept the challenges that aging presents—we can prepare for them and, in doing so, significantly improve the experience our families will have if and when these challenges arrive.

Questions to discuss with your spouse and/or partner

1. What in my mind would constitute behavior concerning enough that I would want someone to step in and help me manage my affairs?

    ....

    ....

    ....

2. If either of us exhibited behavior like this, what actions would we each want the other to take? (regarding managing finances, finding care, living arrangements, etc.) What would each of us be comfortable with the other doing in this situation?

    ....

    ....

    ....

3. How would we want to tell our children? What actions would we want our children to take if both of us were experiencing cognitive difficulties?

    ....

    ....

    ....

Questions to discuss with your advisor

1. According to my documents, who will be in charge if my mental capacity diminishes?

    ....

    ....

2. Who decides when my mental capacity is diminishing? How would my incapacity be demonstrated? What would happen if I disagreed at the time? What options would the people I have named to help me have in that situation?

    ....

    ....

    ....

    ....

3. If you noticed changes in my behavior that you were concerned about, what would you do? If you were ever concerned by instructions I was giving you regarding my financial situation, how would you handle that?

    ....

    ....

4.   Can I name people now so that you would be able to
     share your concerns with them and get them involved?

....

....

5.   Can we invite my successor trustee and/or named at-
     torney-in-fact to a meeting, so they can meet you and
     understand how this might all play out and what they
     might be called on to do one day?

....

....

6.   Are my assets titled appropriately? Are they where they
     need to be so that my successor trustee will be able to
     assume his or her role without difficulty?

....

....

7.   Will the institutions where my assets are custodied
     accept my estate planning forms, or do they have
     forms of their own that we should fill out to make it
     easier for the people I have named to take over?

....

....

Questions to discuss with your children

1. What, in your minds, would be the ideal way for the
    situation to play out if one of us started exhibiting
    cognitive decline? How would you all hope that we
    would act? What role would you like to play, if any?

    ....
    ....
    ....
    ....
    ....
    ....
    ....

2. What kind of behavior do you all think would require
    us to have someone step in and help us manage our
    affairs?

    ....
    ....
    ....
    ....
    ....

3.   If we begin to experience problems, how will you
     all come to agreement that action is needed? How
     long do you think you would need to see us exhibit
     concerning behavior before you would all agree that
     something would need to be done?

....

....

....

....

....

....

....

4.   If we are exhibiting this behavior, but don't see it
     ourselves and don't agree when you raise it with us that
     there is a problem, what do we hope you would do in
     that situation?

....

....

....

5.   What can we do now, as a family, to make it easier on all of us if this arises? (Spelling out roles, identifying behavioral triggers, deciding which doctors and advisors will be contacted, etc.)

....

....

....

....

6.   If this issue arose, what is the first step we would want you all to take?

....

....

....

....

....

CHAPTER EIGHT

A GOOD DEATH

....

Finding the Right Balance Between What We Can and Cannot Control

The culture we live in celebrates action, beauty, and productivity more than it celebrates contemplation and wisdom. Understandably, most of us are not in the habit of spending time thinking about unpleasant topics, so when we look ahead to our later years, we minimize thoughts of slowing down and aging bodies, and likely avoid entirely thoughts about death. No one wants to dwell on his or her own mortality, or worse yet the mortality of a loved one. "We are like children who cover their eyes in a game of hide-and-seek and think that no one can see them," writes Sogyal Rinpoche in *The Tibetan Book of Living and Dying*.[63]

Yet the subject of death has not always been as removed as it is today, nor as abstract: within the last century, the majority of people died in their homes and there was considerably less fear and stigma attached to the process. In contrast, nowadays 60% of Americans die in acute-care hospitals, 20% in nursing homes, and only 20% at home.[64] In the course of people's regular lives, it is not common for them to deal face to face with the dying.

One of the most impactful things we can do in the wealth-advisory field is work with clients and the families they will leave behind to facilitate discussions of how the final years (including death) will unfold. One of our primary motivations is to bring clients peace of mind, and it is in this kind of difficult emotional work that we can bring them a sense of peace that will be deep and lasting—one that will not only positively impact them, but also truly matter to the generations that follow.

As you will see, one of the very kindest things a person can do for his or her family—for both financial well-being and emotional peace of mind—is to contemplate how he or she would like the end of life to unfold and to communicate these wishes openly, honestly, and uniformly with every family member who might have an emotional investment in the outcome. "Families that have conversations between parents and adult children have a much better death than those who don't," says professional family facilitator Bob Mauterstock. "Families break apart if there's not some form of communication between generations."

Let's look more closely at why this conversation is so very hard, and why it must be undertaken.

A critical topic, universally shunned

A national organization called The Conversation Project, which seeks to help people talk about their wishes for end-of-life care, discovered in a 2013 survey that while 90% of people say talking with family about death is important, only 27% have actually done so. The statistics are remarkably similar for people who say they think it is important to put their wishes in writing

(87%) versus the number who have actually done so (23%).[65]

In fact, we learned through our interviews that there is almost an inverse correlation between vibrant later living and proactive discussions about the end of life. The healthier and happier older people feel, the less likely they are to contemplate their own aging or dying, or to communicate their wishes to family members about how those stages should unfold. Of our interviewees, less than 10% had had these detailed conversations with their loved ones. The few who had taken this important step had done so either because they were in the medical field or because they had lived through a close family member's death and were awakened to the necessity of discussing these topics.

Why is there such a deep aversion to doing something everyone knows is so critical? We discovered in our interviews that there are many reasons for this avoidance:

- **Irrelevance:** If people feel young and healthy, death doesn't seem imminent or relevant. One of our most active interviewees has not planned ahead even though he has known several people in his life who died young and unexpectedly. "I just haven't gone there yet," he said.

- **Fear of a jinx:** Consciously or unconsciously, people feel as if opening the topic of death will invite some sort of jinx on them. "Even talking about death is considered morbid," writes Sogyal Rinpoche, "and many people believe that simply mentioning death is to risk wishing it upon ourselves."[66]

- **Uncertainty:** People often have trouble sorting out conflicting emotions about what they really want—and this can seem like too daunting and depressing a project even to begin. This is compounded by the unpredictability of death itself—if you don't know when or how it will happen, there is a sense that there isn't much you can plan for.

- **It's all taken care of:** People often believe that if their legal documents are in place, they have already taken care of the planning they need to do. "Our estate docs are all up to date, so we're good" is a familiar refrain.

- **Focusing on the after-death period:** If people contemplate death at all, they tend to think more about their funeral and eulogy than about the time leading up to death and their wishes for the process of death itself. Yet it's often in this period, when difficult decisions need to be made, that the risk to family harmony is greatest.

- **Desire to avoid stress:** "Elder parents don't want to worry their children ('I don't want to worry them by bringing up the subject that I'm going to die') and adult children don't want their parents to think they're going to die," explains Ellen Goodman, Director of The Conversation Project. As Sarah Putnam explained to us, the irony is that many people fear that planning ahead and discussing it will create conflict among their children, "but if you're having that fear, there's a certainty that there's going to be conflict later!"

- **I'll be gone, anyway:** Some believe it is the children's job to figure out the details, even though this is a devastating legacy to leave behind. Mauterstock minced no words in talking about this aspect of older people's reasoning: "If they don't take responsibility and step up to the plate, they're wishing their families into chaos."

- **Too time-consuming:** Communicating about this topic the right way requires clarifying your own thoughts and then sharing these uniformly with your loved ones, either in a letter or in a family gathering where everyone can be present and hear the same version of events. All of that requires setting aside time dedicated to this purpose. A conversation this serious and wide-ranging feels out of place around the Thanksgiving dinner table.

- **Out of character:** Perhaps the matriarch or patriarch has always been the stalwart type—the rock—and does not like to express a sense of vulnerability or decline. One of our interviewees had this mindset: a diligent worker, his job was to support his family financially and emotionally, to be in charge. Now in his 80s, he finds that he has neglected to plan or talk much about the future. "What I've told you, I've never told my kids. They view us as very self-sustaining," he explained. "That's the world we created. Communication with my family is not my strong suit."

- **It's never come up!** Occasionally, there is no active reason why the conversation hasn't happened. It's just one of the many things that have not yet been discussed in otherwise busy lives.

Yes, there are a number of good reasons why the end of life is rarely discussed. Unfortunately, these are dwarfed in significance by the reason why it can't be ignored. All of the wealth management advice in the world is useless if family members and their relationships with one another crumble under the weight of a crisis that might have been avoided. And the last years of life present many opportunities for crisis, fueled by the combustible mix of overwhelming emotion—grief, stress, changing power dynamics in a family—and a constant barrage of decisions that need to be made: Where is the best medical care? What is the best living arrangement? What would Mom really want in this situation?

It is only through communicating your wishes to your family that you can ensure that they will have clarity about what you want and will not have to debate this and arrive at consensus in a time of crisis, when they will likely be in the throes of grief. "A crisis is a terrible time to learn," says Ellen Goodman, Director of The Conversation Project. "One of the things that does happen when people come to the end of their life is, if they haven't had the conversation with their family, we know their children can get into incredible problems. There's conflict about what to do. It can tear families apart, and that is the worst legacy you could possibly leave."

Authoring your own death experience

But first, before we discuss how contemplating your death experience can help your family, let's talk about how it can help you. None of us can choose whether to die, but aging, as opposed to sudden death, presents us with a gift—the gift of authoring our death experience as the final developmental stage of our lives.

When the British neurologist and bestselling author Oliver Sacks was facing death from liver cancer at age 80, he was not yet ready for the end. Having spent decades without a romantic partner, he had only recently found love. He was in the middle of writing numerous books and still had an enduring zest for life and adventure. But he was forced to face reality.

"Over the last few days, I have been able to see my life as from a great altitude, as a sort of landscape, and with a deepening sense of the connection of all its parts," he wrote in his book *Gratitude*. "This does not mean I am finished with life. On the contrary, I feel intensely alive, and I want and hope in the time that remains to deepen my friendships, to say farewell to those I love, to write more, to travel if I have the strength, to achieve new levels of understanding and insight."[67]

"And now, weak, short of breath, my once firm muscles melted away by cancer," Sacks writes later in the book, "I find my thoughts, increasingly, not on the supernatural or spiritual but on what is meant by living a good and worthwhile life—achieving a peace within oneself."[68] Without this clear assessment and acceptance of his situation, Sacks would miss the chance to see his life holistically and to take pride in how well he has been living it.

Gloria—the 88-year-old painter and designer from Arlington—also chose to live with the reality of her own eventual death. Always a deep thinker, she felt the presence of death in her life from an early age. For a reason she does not understand, as a child she had believed she would die when she turned 27. When that failed to happen, she thought perhaps it would be at age 72. Now nearing 90, she says she has thought about death so much that she has no fears about it: "I've done a lot of planning. I've always been curious about death."

This perspective has led her to embrace life fully, to think ahead, and to assume that she can have some control over whatever situation she might find herself in. "I think that the worst thing to do is to start making wrong assumptions," she explained. "The best way is, if you want to do something, expect that you're going to be able to do it. This goes for dying too."

When Gloria's husband was diagnosed with a slow-acting and painful form of inoperable cancer, she says that he believed "it was his moment to go, and he was going to take it." He chose not to see himself as a victim and began to refuse food. Gloria remembers his last days in their home as days filled with muted sadness, moments of tenderness, constant music, and the sense that her husband—while dying—was exerting some control over his life. That is also how she hopes to go when the time comes.

While there is no single, perfect way to adjust to the reality of death, there is your way—and everyone has the right and responsibility to make that way known to others. "There is a good enough death," writes Ann Neumann, after analyzing the many complexities of dying in America in her book *The Good Death*. "It is possible to look at death in the face, to know how it will come, to accept its inevitability. There are many kinds of good enough death, each specific to the person dying. As they wish, as best they can."[69]

Interestingly, studies have found that you cannot count on medical professionals to take the lead in prodding you to be realistic about death. Dr. VJ Periyakoil of The Stanford Letter Project surveyed more than 1,000 medical residents and found that most resisted talking with ill patients about what was important to them in their final days (in particular if the patient's ethnicity differed from their own). Of those surveyed, 99.99% reported facing barriers to frank conversations, and 86% rated those barriers as very challenging.[70]

The Serious Illness Conversation Guide, created by Ariadne Labs, a research group founded by Atul Gawande to promote a better standard of care, attempts to remedy this problem by equipping physicians with a simple roadmap to follow as they attempt to lead these conversations.[71] The guide, as well as the increasing attention that this topic has recently garnered through Gawande's book and several others about the end of life, has had some impact within the medical community, with more physicians feeling better prepared to initiate and facilitate these conversations. But we have a long way to go before an open and thoughtful discussion about death will be a routine and practiced part of the standard end-of-life medical experience. And until that day, the conclusion is clear: if you want to have a say in how you die, you must be brave and start that conversation yourself.

Starting the conversation does several things. It first allows you to become familiar with questions that will take on significance during your end-of-life experience and to contemplate your answers when you can think rationally, when you are not in the grip of fear, instinctively trying to do all you can to delay the inevitable. Also, contemplating these issues will get you into the habit of doing this on a regular basis, which is good practice for the true experience at the end of life, when you will need to check in and reassess priorities regularly as the situation, your prognosis, and your capacities evolve: What matters to me the most now? What can be done to enhance the quality, not just the quantity, of my life now, at this stage? For example, if your top priority is to attend a grandchild's graduation in two weeks, perhaps you should forego a treatment that might prolong your life by several weeks but would make attendance impossible. If you get into the habit now of thinking through and clearly articulating what will matter most to you, when the time comes you will be practiced at this and will not need to wait for your medical professional or family members to ask.

Facing death helps you prioritize now

Besides authoring your own death experience, there are other benefits to actively contemplating your mortality. The awareness that your time is finite prompts you to think more deeply about how you will spend it; it encourages you to apply yourself to whatever you will find most meaningful, that will make you feel that you have used your time well. "The transience of life is the engine of its meaning," writes journalist Andrew Solomon. "Believing that may be our only way to make the best of a bad situation—but what a way it is."[72]

After Steve Jobs, the founder of Apple, discovered he had incurable cancer, the knowledge of his mortality sharpened his focus, instantly helping him prioritize. "Remembering that I'll be dead soon is the most important tool I've ever encountered to help me make the big choices in life," he told students at his alma mater, Stanford University, in 2005.[73] This idea resonated deeply with a wide audience: the video and transcript of Jobs' speech has been viewed and shared millions of times.

A gift for those you leave behind

If you remain unconvinced that you'll derive any benefits from contemplating your death and how you would like the end of your life to unfold, don't do it for yourself; do it for those you will leave behind. Facing death with a sense of practicality, equanimity, and clarity is the ultimate gift you can leave your children, friends, and loved ones. Children especially want to know what their parents want, and being able to execute on a parent's wishes leaves children with a deep sense of contentment and peace of mind. It is in this peace of mind that your ultimate legacy lies: the ability for you to be remembered fondly, and with gratitude.

Also, by being clear about what you want, you are doing what you can to ensure that family discord will not erupt upon your passing. It is much easier for your children to be in agreement about what to do when you have articulated your wishes openly and clearly. Surely it is better for everyone to have your passing leave others with thoughts of peace and gratitude, rather than resentment and discord?

We heard several stories from our interviewees that drove home this point. One involved Debbie's mother, Faith, whom you might remember from the last chapter as being very clear about wanting to live in her home as she aged. It turns out that Faith was also very clear about how she wanted the end of her life to unfold. Debbie shared with us how this came to be.

It started when Debbie's father, Frank, became ill. Standing at over 6 feet, Frank had a head of white hair, and a can-do attitude. In his 70s he appeared in good health, and it seemed to his family that he would live forever. When he was diagnosed with a rapidly growing terminal cancer, Frank went into deep denial. Returning to his yellow clapboard house on the Jersey Shore after a particularly sobering doctor's visit, he looked up at the house and declared that it was time for him to give it a new paint job. Debbie cast a sideways glance at her sister: her father had clearly not absorbed the doctor's prognosis.

But there was no turning away from reality. Frank's health

continued to deteriorate, which meant that the family had to accept the inevitability of his death. Eventually hospice was called into their home. At first Debbie's parents resisted this, but the family soon learned how powerful and peaceful these final moments could be. "We had some control over how we cared for him and treated him," Debbie said.

After Frank's death, Faith decided that she too wanted to die at home with her family around her. Previously she had expected to go into assisted living, but she became inspired by seeing family members care for her husband in their home: they lit candles in his room, washed the surfaces down with rosemary spray so it smelled fresh, cleaned his sheets every other day, and generally created a soothing, intimate atmosphere.

"I'm just telling you all right now I want to be carried feet first in a body bag out my front door," Faith declared to her four children. This idea of carrying her out became something of a family joke, but when the time actually came—and she was indeed carried out of her own home, feet first—the children felt a sense of achievement at having managed to meet her wishes. They knew her favorite song, her favorite part of the Bible, and had already picked out her casket at the funeral home. "It makes it easy for people you leave behind if you have clear wishes," Debbie said. The social worker who visited them on the last day of her mother's life was astonished; he said it was the first time he had ever worked with a family who was so on target and harmonious.

"None of us were trying to be the hero in my parents' story," Debbie added. "We were participants. They were the elders."

Having a plan that allowed them to face reality head-on, without conflict, brought Debbie and her family great peace. Debbie had heard many horror stories about siblings arguing during the last weeks of a parent's life, but she and her siblings managed to avoid any territorial fights. Faith's clear wishes, and her vocal (and humorous) insistence on them, provided a clear roadmap for the siblings to follow. This kind of clarity is key in helping siblings avoid the types of conflicts that are common when their parents face decline and death.

People react to death in many different ways; one sibling might want extraordinary measures taken, whereas another might think things should be left to follow a natural course. "It's really hard for a lot of families to make these decisions and work together," Debbie explained. "There are so many families who freak out." If even one sibling disagrees with the others, it can cause huge problems. For Debbie, feeling unified with her brother and sisters was an experience that transformed her parents' passing into a surprisingly healing experience. "I think we were lucky that as siblings we could come together," she said. "My mother really pushed for that. She always told us, 'You only have each other.' We'd been told since we were little that we were supposed to take care of each other. It was clearly established that the children would work together."

The goal is to have peaceful final moments

When you have done the work to accept death and to communicate your wishes clearly to your loved ones, you are far more likely to be able to experience the kind of final interactions that are most meaningful to family. These will be the moments people replay in their minds when you are gone; you are giving the people you leave behind the gift of being able to think of you peacefully. When you are with a person who has a "good" death, it is those good moments that you remember.

Our interviewee Peggy and her family were able to use the experiences from when their father died to guide them when their mother, Isabelle, faced the very end of her life. During Isabelle's final weeks, Peggy appreciated the clarity she had about her mother's wishes. "Making plans and organizing relieves stress for me, so I was able to say to my mom that I needed to do that, and I could make a joke out of it," Peggy explained. Isabelle was very specific about not wanting to live in a disabled state, which to her meant not being put on oxygen permanently. The family even video-taped a long discussion about her decisions regarding intubation, which turned out to be incredibly helpful later when decisions became high stakes and stressful. "She considered that her gift to us," said Peggy, "because she'd put herself in a position where it was easy for us to take care of her."

Even so, they did have to interpret her mother's wishes: as she lay close to dying, one sister and a brother wanted her to be kept alive a little longer, so they could come and see her one last time. Because the family knew that this decision was a short-term one and were clear and united about what Isabelle ultimately wanted, they were able to make this choice without too much agonizing.

"How nice it is when the person makes it clear that they are okay with death, tired of interventions," Peggy said. "When they are ready to go and they don't seem to be afraid, it's a whole different situation. You're so much more able to say your last words to someone."

Being accepting helps others accept too

You have to be willing to let people go. Donald sat in his

office at the business school where he teaches and talked about the recent death of his mother. Despite daily calls to ensure himself of her well-being, when he was traveling in Rome his mother took a fall and hit her head. By the time he returned to the U.S., doctors had already put in a pacemaker and installed her in the assisted-living facility of her retirement home.

He insisted that she could, and should, return to her own apartment, despite the safety risks. "You need to be willing to fight for what you want," he said, frowning. But when his mother got pneumonia, she was sent once again to intensive care and then pumped full of antibiotics. Over the next several months, she was in and out of the hospital and various rehab facilities. Donald felt torn. He was playing the cheerleader, trying to keep his mother's spirits up, but he was also trying to navigate the tricky balance between the march toward ever-increasing medical intervention and her wishes to die a minimally invasive death.

What helped him ultimately was that his mother let him know she was ready to go. "At the end she said, 'I'm tired. I've had a great life, I wouldn't have traded the last three years for any-thing,'" he explained. Donald struggled to reconcile this with his own instinct to fight and do more for her. He remembers being moved by his mother's rabbi's advice: "This isn't about you, this is about her." Reflecting on this now, Donald says, "I had to shift from being the boss and handling everything to understanding her. I had to honor her wishes."

He smiled. "She had a good end," he said. "I had a good end!" He has now changed his own living will as a result of experiencing this with his mother. His new philosophy is: when it's time to go, it's time to go.

How hospice can help

In his book *Being Mortal*, Atul Gawande explores at length the various choices people make about where to spend their last days and suggests hospice care as a kinder and gentler alternative to a hospital. Hospice brings professionals to the home and minimizes medical intervention; it is rising in popularity as people seek to have a less medicalized end. According to The Institute for Palliative Care, nearly two of every five people who died in the United States in 2008 were under the care of a hospice program at the time of their death.[74]

"Spending one's final days in an ICU because of terminal illness is for most people a kind of failure," Gawande writes. "You lie attached to a ventilator, your every organ shutting down, your mind teetering on delirium and permanently beyond realizing that you will never leave this borrowed, fluorescent place. The end comes with no chance for you to have said good-bye or 'It's okay' or 'I'm sorry' or 'I love you.'"[75]

Gawande reveals in his book that when his own father was facing the end, his family was reluctant to choose hospice care, as it seemed to represent a sort of giving in, a hastening of the death process. But he soon realized that it was just the opposite—and statistics prove it. On average, people live longer in hospice care than in the ICU, and their experiences are far less traumatic. In one study, patients who enrolled in hospice care suffered less, were more physically capable, and could interact better with others. Also, after their deaths, family members were less likely to experience persistent major depression.

In Debbie's case, choosing hospice allowed the deaths of both her father, Frank, and her mother, Faith, to feel intimate and personal. That closeness at the end is powerful, and can even seem magical. "It makes the end of life and the miracle of death mirror the miracle of birth," Debbie said. "People have lost the spirituality in living and dying. I believe hospice gives that back to you." She and her siblings did not feel they were sentencing their parents to death, rather that they were giving them what they wanted in the best possible way. "When they're gone, it validates your love and respect for that person," Debbie said.

Under hospice care, death is less mysterious and there is more open communication about its realities. A good hospice-care nurse is able to alert others when someone is getting close to the end, giving family and loved ones a two to three day window of time. "Unless we have been there, we often don't realize that, like birth, death—be it from illness or age—comes in stages," writes Margaret Hathaway in her 2016 *Taproot* article about the death of her father at her remote farm. "[T]here is work being done, the last ordering of a life. And it can be participatory work; death does not have to be relegated to a final, lonely solo. In making the dying feel safe and loved, we make their transition less scary, and we ease the wild-eyed animal fear of death."[76] People have the chance to make decisions and say good-bye, without pressure from the medical establishment to prolong life at any cost.

The impact on Debbie's own outlook has been profound. "The aging process and the death process is difficult, but you can do it right," she said. "It makes it easy for the people who are left behind because you're doing what the person wanted." She paused to think for a moment. "Don't just say, 'Do what you want, I won't be there.' No—but your kids will. Think about what you are asking your family to take on."

As a result of her experience, she has now recorded a video of her wishes for her own death experience and intends to share it with her children so that, when the time comes, they will know exactly what she wants and what they can do to help her. "I'm not afraid of death anymore; I'm not worried about it," she said. "That's the other thing that it teaches you when you are present when someone goes."

Why details are all-important

Journalist Ann Neumann wrote the book *The Good Death* after she became tormented by the question of whether she had denied her father a good death. After he became ill, she quit her job and moved in with him, nursing him tenderly for the last months of his life. They became very close, and even though the job was grueling and often overwhelming, she felt she was taking on an important responsibility.

However, the end of life presents its own confusing issues. Her father was insistent that he wanted to die at home, and Neumann wanted to grant him that wish. But the end was drawn-out and difficult, and she did not understand the stages of death or how to help him manage his pain; eventually she panicked and called 911. EMTs rushed him to the hospital, where he died hours later, and she felt a profound sense of failure. He had been clear about his wishes, but together they had failed to be clear enough about the specifics.[77]

The devil is truly in the details. You may have made the best-laid plans, but you must be sure that they sync up with the laws in your home state. Video journalist Sarah Putnam filmed a woman named Jane speaking about the end of her husband's life.[78] He had been ill for a long time, and they had spoken in detail about his wishes for a natural, non-invasive death and had completed all the necessary paperwork. As the end neared, Jane was at home with her family, playing board games, while her husband rested in their bed. At one point, she went in to check on him and found him lying still and peacefully, no longer breathing. Jane called 911—not to revive him but to acknowledge his passing.

That's when things started to go wrong: when the EMTs arrived, they pulled him off the bed and put him on the floor, pounding on him to try to get his heart beating again. "I said no! He's DNR!" Jane recalls in the video. But the Do Not Resuscitate paperwork was with his doctor and at the hospital, and the rules in her state were that she had to have them in hand or else the EMTs were required to act. "It seemed so disrespectful. I'm sure at that point it made no difference to him. He was gone. The body was certainly not of use to him anymore, but it was to me. He was still my honey."

Jane regrets not understanding the intricacies of the system and is left with lingering sadness about her husband's last moments. "I thought that because we were well-prepared, this wouldn't happen," she says. "I thought we had done it right."

Starting the conversation

Understandably, most people are reluctant to talk about end of life, but we found in our interviews that people were less intimidated when they had been touched by death and were therefore already alerted to the issue. One of our interviewees, Mary Jane, had worked in hospice care for many years (before the practice was even licensed), and she and her children often talked about her work. Her younger son showed special interest, often asking her, "How do you do what you do?" "It would kick off the conversation," Mary Jane said. "I've committed my working life to helping people die peacefully, so I think that spoke very loudly."

When it came time to talk with her children more specifically about her own wishes for end of life, her youngest son was the first to "get it"—he had had a terminally ill friend who committed assisted suicide, so he understood the benefits of clarity and decisiveness. Both Mary Jane and her husband now feel that everything is squared away and that their children are on board with their wishes. "As my mother used to say, 'If you don't tell me, I won't know!'" Mary Jane said, laughing.

Our interviewee Paul says he and his wife have talked a lot about death because of his work over the years in medicine, understanding biological processes: "We're pretty fatalistic about it," he explained. They have a church community with whom they've had many conversations in a small group setting. They talk about plans for memorial services and burials, and they even went with another couple to buy plots at a local cemetery. "We've taken advantage of church-related connectivity, and that's helped us talk about it with our kids too," Paul said.

Nonetheless, he recognizes that this is a difficult topic. "There's a kind of inevitable anxiety that emerges, even though it may sound like we've got things pretty tied together," he said. "When things do go wrong, how is it going to work out? That discomfort about the unknown is a real factor as you get older. You know it's inevitable, but what will it be and how will you deal with it? I think that's a normal process about being honest about what's going to happen."

Wrapping your head around the topic

Death is at once epic and rather mundane. "Both despair and euphoria about death are an evasion. Death is neither depressing nor exciting; it is simply a fact of life," writes Sogyal Rinpoche.[79] The best way to handle this difficult topic may well be to treat it as you treat the unpleasant medical check-ups that you need as you age: no one troops off joyfully to have a colonoscopy or a mammogram, yet they know it's necessary, and they get it done. A baseline plan that is continually updated about living will wishes, goals for the end of life, funeral plans, and a burial plot is simply another necessary element of a long and full life.

"No one ever really has control," Atul Gawande writes. "Physics and biology and accident ultimately have their way in our lives. But the point is that we are not helpless either. Courage is the strength to recognize both realities."[80]

There is some comfort in knowing that, though ultimately we all face the same end, we can choose to make that end easier on ourselves and on others by embracing clarity around our previously unspoken wishes. Perhaps it's best to think like the Dalai Lama, who espouses a practical attitude toward death. "Knowing that I cannot escape it, I see no point in worrying about it," he says. "Yet death is unpredictable: we do not know when or how it will take place. So it is only sensible to take certain precautions before it actually happens."[81]

Questions to ponder and discuss about end of life

1. What do I want my end-of-life experience to be like?
    What matters most to me?

    ....

    ....

    ....

    ....

    ....

2. Have I articulated my end-of-life wishes in detail? (If
    not, use one of the frameworks listed in the resource
    box at the end of this chapter as a guide.)

    ....

    ....

3. Do I know my spouse's end-of-life wishes? (If not, have
    your spouse do the same.)

    ....

    ....

    ....

    ....

4. How would I like my children to describe my end-of-
    life process after I'm gone? Will the plans that I have
    articulated make that possible?

    ....

    ....

5. Have I anticipated conflicts that might arise among my
    loved ones, and if so, is there a way to address them
    proactively?

    ....

    ....

6. Have I communicated my wishes openly, clearly, and
    consistently to all of my loved ones who might have an
    emotional stake in the outcome?

    ....

    ....

7. Have I taken care of the details, so that when the time
    comes my wishes can be followed? (e.g. Do I have a
    copy of my DNR available to be given to EMTs if
    necessary? Is one on file at my local hospital?, etc.)

    ....

    ....

Resources for contemplating and recording end-of-life wishes

Five Wishes (www.agingwithdignity.org/)

The Conversation Project's end-of-life conversation starter kit (theconversationproject.org/wp-content/uploads/2017/02/ConversationProject-ConvoStarterKit-English.pdf)

Stanford Medicine Letter Project, Dear Doctor/Advanced Directives form (dear-doc.appspot.com/html/adv.html)

The LastingMatters Organizer: Where loved ones find what matters most by Barbara Bates Sedoric (www.lastingmatters.com/)

If you are ill now, use Ariadne Labs' *Serious Illness Conversation Guide* and share it with your doctor (www.ariadnelabs.org/wp-content/uploads/sites/2/2015/08/Serious-Illness-Conversation-Guide-5.22.15.pdf)

Chapter Nine
Getting Started

....

How to Implement This Now in Your Own Family

If you've read this far and have been answering the questions in each chapter along the way, you are likely far down the road toward ensuring that the legacy you leave behind will be positive and lasting.

If you haven't answered the questions, now is the time to start. What can you do today so that you and your family members can share positive stories like the ones in this book? What can you put in place now so that your children will express the gratitude and sense of peace that we heard from our interviewees whose parents took these steps?

1. Commit. Make it a gift to your children to act out the following plan. Using the chapter questions as a roadmap, dedicate a vacation to thinking through these questions, first alone and then with your spouse. Use the lines in the question boxes as well as the Notes pages at the end of this book to keep track of your thoughts. At first you may have more questions than answers, but taking uninterrupted time to reflect on these issues and talking them through will allow you to make

significant headway in clarifying your thinking. There will be plenty of instances along the way when you'll want to stop—remember all of the reasons people gave us for never wanting to contemplate these topics? But, if and when you feel like that, steel yourself and tell yourself that, though there are many things in life you can't control, this isn't one of them, and that's a gift.

2. Next, find a way to communicate your thoughts to your children. There are a host of ways—in writing, in video, or in person in a family discussion. If you decide to go the route of a family meeting, work with an advisor to facilitate this discussion or use one of the resources we have listed below to help you structure the agenda so that it goes well. Whatever method you choose to communicate your thoughts, make sure that the end result will be that everyone has a clear and consistent understanding of your wishes. You may not be able to head off all conflicts among your children, but you can at least ensure that lack of clarity on your part does not fuel a disagreement. Your children may not all agree with your wishes, but at least they will not need to argue among themselves about what you intended.

Giving the gift of clarity may take a month, a year, or more, but set that as your goal and take the first step today.

Resources for hosting a legacy-focused family meeting

Passing the Torch: Critical Conversations With Your Adult Children by Bob Mauterstock

A Handbook for Conducting Effective Multigenerational Family Meetings about Business and Wealth by Dennis Jaffe and Stacy Allred (dennisjaffe.com/download/a-hand-book-for-conducting-effective-multigenerational-family-meetings-about-business-and-wealth/)

21/64 Toolkits (2164.net/store)

SECTION THREE

The Questions We Asked Our Interviewees

···

We heard from many of our interviewees that they found the process of answering the questions we asked very moving. For many, this was the first time they had contemplated these topics, and doing so prompted them to have a conversation with their spouse and/or children about their thoughts.

With the hope that you might be similarly inspired, we have included the questions we asked below, grouped into the same categories we used in our interviews:

Later-life living

1. How do you define successful aging?

2. What do you think are the most important factors for aging well?

3. What aspects of your life have been most helpful to you as you have gotten older? Why? Describe them for us.

4. What gives you meaning in your day-to-day life?

5. Do you have a philosophy of life that you live by?

6. What are your greatest joys day to day? And over the long term?

7. What are your biggest challenges?

8. Do you feel you have more responsibility versus when you were younger, or less?

9. Does your life bring you into contact with people of different age groups? How?

10. What is your attitude toward the unknown? Adventure? Risk taking?

11. Do you feel your personality has changed over the last 10 years? If so, how?

12. Are there any aspects of your personality that you think have helped or hindered you as you age?

13. Has the way you spend your time evolved over the last 10 years? How so? Tell us about any transitions you went through and how you managed those. Have you let anything go or added anything to your life?

14. When you think of the process of aging gracefully, what role models do you find yourself reflecting upon?

15. How was your parents' aging experience? What did you learn from that? Is there anything you hope to replicate? To do differently?

Aging and wealth

1. Has your relationship to (or attitude toward) your wealth changed as you have gotten older? How so?

2. Have you evolved in how you have chosen to use your wealth? How so?

3. What have been the most rewarding ways in which you have used your wealth as you have gotten older?

4. When you think of the vision you had of yourself as an older person, has your wealth made that more or less possible? In what way?

5. If you are a grandparent, what has been the most fulfilling thing you've done as a grandparent?

End of life

1. If you have had to deal with your own parents' or friends' end-of-life experiences, what have you learned from these? What have you admired? Is there anything you would do differently?

2. Have you done much planning for your own death experience? Why or why not?

3. Have you discussed your wishes with your family? Why or why not?

Reflecting on aging

1. What were your expectations of aging? How has reality been different? What has been most surprising?

2. What are your strategies for coping with the aging process? Do you have any fears about aging? How do you manage those fears?

3. Was there any action you took, any change in your life, that enabled you to age more contentedly that you would recommend to others?

4. Knowing what you know now about aging, is there any advice you would give to your younger self?

Aging Inspiration

....

Uplifting Films and Websites about Aging

Films

Alive Inside: A Story of Music and Memory (2014) - Documentary

An awe-inspiring look at how familiar music has the power to "reawaken" people with even severe dementia and bring them back to themselves, their identities, and even their memories. Watch this if you have someone with dementia in your life.

Best Exotic Marigold Hotel (2011)

Perhaps a little Hollywoodified, but still an uplifting tale of British retirees who decamp to India. Worth watching for the stellar cast and characters alone, but the entrancing backdrop of India and how it shakes them all out of their comfortable routines is an added bonus.

Buena Vista Social Club (1999) - Documentary

Wim Wender's documentary about aging Cuban musicians who

were brought out of obscurity to record a new album spurred
a revival of '50s Cuban music and a resurgence of many of the
musicians' careers. Worth watching for the terrific soundtrack
and the sense of justice in seeing long-forgotten musical talents
emerge again for a much-deserved day in the sun.

Cyber-Seniors (2014) - Documentary
A funny and poignant look at how a group of teens partnered
with seniors to teach them about technology and getting online.
It's heartwarming to see how these two groups help each other—the teens find a purpose in using their technological savvy
to open worlds for the seniors, and the seniors experience the
best that technological connectedness has to offer, from reunions
with distant relatives to a late-blooming career as a YouTube
sensation.

On Golden Pond (1981)
This classic is worth watching less for Henry Fonda's curmud-
geonly Norman than for Katharine Hepburn's stalwartly optimistic portrayal of his wife, Ethel. Both the character of Ethel
and the actress herself at this late stage in her career demonstrate
what it means to age with positivity, bravery, and agency.

The Lady in Number 6 (2013) - Documentary
An incredibly uplifting story of 109-year-old Holocaust survivor
and concert pianist, Alice Herz-Sommer, as she reflects on her
life and shares her joy for living. Watch this if you are feeling
down about aging or anything else for that matter.

Quartet (2012)

A quiet comedy about life and relationships in a retirement home for professional musicians. Beautiful music and setting throughout, and a hopeful message that it is never too late to right past wrongs.

Young@Heart (2007) - Documentary

The story of the Young@Heart chorus (with members in their 70s-90s) as they prepare new rock songs, from Coldplay to James Brown, for an upcoming concert and persevere through health crises and other heart-wrenching difficulties. It's thrilling to see how they pull it all together, and it will leave you feeling just like an audience member at the final rousing concert who said, "I'm never going to complain about being too old and too tired again!"

Websites

encore.org
legacyproject.human.cornell.edu
lifereimagined.aarp.org
longevity.stanford.edu
roadscholar.org

Recommended Reading

On Healthy, Engaged, and Purposeful Later-Life Living

The Blue Zones: 9 Lessons for Living Longer from the People Who've Lived the Longest *by Dan Buettner*

Younger Next Year: Live Strong, Fit, and Sexy—Until You're 80 and Beyond *and* Younger Next Year: The Exercise Program: Use the Power of Exercise to Reverse Aging and Stay Strong, Fit, and Sexy *by Chris Crowley and Henry S. Lodge*

Life Reimagined: The Science, Art, and Opportunity of Midlife *by Barbara Bradley Hagerty*

Live Long, Die Short: A Guide to Authentic Health and Successful Aging *by Roger Landy*

Counterclockwise: Mindful Health and the Power of Possibility *by Ellen J. Langer*

The Art of Aging: A Doctor's Prescription for Wellbeing *by Sherwin B. Nuland*

Aging Well: Surprising Guideposts to a Happier Life from the Landmark Harvard Study of Adult Development *by George E. Vaillant*

Healthy Aging: A Lifelong Guide to Your Well-Being *by Andrew Weil*

ON THE SPIRITUAL ASPECTS OF AGING

The Gift of Years: Growing Older Gracefully *by Joan Chittister*

Aging as a Spiritual Practice: A Contemplative Guide to Growing Older and Wiser *by Lewis Richmond*

From AGE-ING to SAGE-ING: A Revolutionary Approach to Growing Older *by Zalman Schachter-Shalomi and Ronald S. Miller*

ON LEGACY

Tuesdays with Morrie: An Old Man, a Young Man, and Life's Greatest Lesson *by Mitch Albom*

Creating the Good Will: The Most Comprehensive Guide to Both the Financial and Emotional Sides of Passing on Your Legacy *by Elizabeth Arnold*

How Will You Measure Your Life? *by Clayton M. Christensen*

Plus the additional resources listed at the end of Chapter Six.

On the End of Life

Being Mortal: Medicine and What Matters in the End *by Atul Gawande*

When Breath Becomes Air *by Paul Kalanathi*

The Good Death: An Exploration of Dying in America *by Ann Neumann*

The Tibetan Book of Living and Dying *by Sogyal Rinpoche*

Plus the additional resources listed at the end of Chapter Eight.

On Empathy/Caregiving For Elders

How We Age: A Doctor's Journey into the Heart of Growing Old *by Marc Agronin*

Don't Give Up on Me! Supporting Aging Parents Successfully: A Daughter's Intimate Memoir *by Jan Simpson*

Another Country: Navigating the Emotional Terrain of Our Elders *by Mary Pipher*

How to Say It to Seniors: Closing the Communication Gap with Our Elders *by David Solie*

AFTERWORD

....

I am grateful to my business partner, friend, and colleague, Coventry ("Covie") Edwards-Pitt, for writing this important book. This is Covie's second book, and, like her first book, *Raised Healthy, Wealthy & Wise* (2014), it breaks new ground.

Covie's book is the first to put into one place all that wealth creators need to address to age well and be satisfied with the legacy they will leave their families once they are gone. In addition to sharing positive stories of our clients and others who are using their resources to design and lead vibrant later lives, Covie addresses three important issues from the perspective of wealth creators and inheritors: (1) the extraordinary opportunities of wealth creators to use family wealth for constructive purposes during the aging process, (2) the importance of making one's plans for the last years of life known well in advance, and (3) the need for wealth creators to communicate with their children, grandchildren, and future generations of the family whom they will never have the opportunity to know.

In our work as advisors to wealthy families, we find that most wealth creators underestimate how curious future generations will be to know the family history and how much those future generations will wish to know about them or decisions they made. Often, our attempts to encourage wealth creators to write about themselves or create an autobiographical video are met with skepticism and embarrassment: "It feels uncomfortable for me to talk about myself and my success. Why will future generations care?" The impetus to act often comes from their children and grandchildren, who realize that an important piece of the family's history will be lost if their parents fail to leave a detailed record. What younger family members seem to care most about is not the story of how the family wealth was created, but the life stories, personal values, and struggles of the senior generation.

The questions in Covie's book are an excellent resource to assist families in capturing the stories that will be meaningful for present and future generations. At first the work involved may seem daunting, but the rewards will become evident as you begin to share your story with family members. Thanks to Covie's thoughtful analysis, my spouse, Sandy, and I have undertaken our own project to think about what we have learned and what lessons we would like to pass on. We hope you will too.

Roy Ballentine
Executive Chairman
Ballentine Partners, LLC

Endnotes

[1] Wan He, Daniel Goodkind, and Paul Kowal, "An Aging World: 2015," *International Population Reports*, (2016). https://www.census.gov/content/dam/Census/library/publications/2016/demo/p95-16-1.pdf.

[2] Mark Mather, Linda A. Jacobsen, and Kelvin M. Pollard, "Aging in the United States," *Population Bulletin* 70, no. 2, (2015): 3. www.prb.org/pdf16/aging-us-population-bulletin.pdf.

[3] Ben Hoyle, "Ben Hoyle: Salman Rushdie unrepentant about Satanic Verses," *History News Network*, October 1, 2008, historynewsnetwork.org/article/55134.

[4] Bruce Grierson, "What if Age Is Nothing but a Mind-Set?" *The New York Times Magazine*, last modified November 9, 2014, www.nytimes.com/2014/10/26/magazine/what-if-age-is-nothing-but-a-mind-set.html?mcubz=0.

[5] Ellen J. Langer, *Counterclockwise: Mindful Health and the Power of Possibility* (New York: Ballantine Books, 2009), 10.

[6] Ibid., 86.

[7] Chris Crowley and Henry S. Lodge, *Younger Next Year for Women: Live Strong, Fit, and Sexy—Until You're 80 and Beyond* (New York: Workman Publishing, 2005), 33.

[8] Chris Crowley, Henry S. Lodge, and Bill Fabrocini, *Younger Next Year: The Exercise Program: Use the Power of Exercise to Reverse Aging and Stay Strong, Fit, and Sexy* (New York: Workman Publishing, 2015), 7-10.

[9] Mitch Albom, *Tuesdays with Morrie: An Old Man, a Young Man, and Life's Greatest Lesson* (New York: Broadway Books, 1997), 35-36.

[10] Viktor E. Frankl, *Man's Search for Meaning* (Boston: Beacon Press, 2006), 86.

[11] Becca R. Levy, Martin D. Slade, Suzanne R. Kunkel, and Stanislav V. Kasl, "Longevity Increased by Positive Self-Perceptions of Aging," *Journal of Personality and Social Psychology* 83, no. 2 (2002), doi: 10.1037//0022-3514.83.2.261.

[12] Icek Ajzen and Martin Fishbein, "The Influence of Attitudes on Behavior," *The Handbook of Attitudes* (2005), web.psych.utoronto.ca/psy320/Required%20readings_files/4-1.pdf.

[13] Amy Morin, "7 Scientifically Proven Benefits of Gratitude That Will Motivate You To Give Thanks Year-Round," *Forbes*, November 23, 2014, www.forbes.com/sites/amymorin/2014/11/23/7-scientifically-proven-benefits-of-gratitude-that- will-motivate-you-to-give-thanks-year-round/#55f74677183c.

[14] Arthur Cropley, "Creative Performance in Older Adults," in *Reflections on Educational Achievement: Papers in Honour of T. Neville Postlethwaite,* eds. Wilfried Bos and Rainer H. Lehmann (Munster, Germany: Waxmann, 1995): 82-85, www.waxmann. com/fileadmin/media/zusatztexte/postlethwaite/cropley.pdf.

[15] Shelley H. Carson, "Creativity and the Aging Brain," *Psychology Today,* March 30, 2009, www.psychologytoday.com/ blog/life-art/200903/creativity-and-the-aging-brain.

[16] Carol S. Dweck, *Mindset: The New Psychology of Success* (New York: Random House, 2006).

[17] Sogyal Rinpoche, *The Tibetan Book of Living and Dying,* eds. Patrick Gaffney and Andrew Harvey (San Francisco: HarperSanFrancisco, 1998), 109.

[18] Clayton M. Christensen, James Allworth, and Karen Dillon, *How Will You Measure Your Life?* (New York: HarperCollins, 2012).

[19] Clifton B. Parker, "Scientific evidence does not support the brain game claims, Stanford scholars say," *Stanford News,* October 20, 2014, news.stanford.edu/news/2014/october/brain-games-carstensen-102014.html.

[20] Lewis Richmond, *Aging as a Spiritual Practice: A Contemplative Guide to Growing Older and Wiser* (New York: Gotham, 2012), 5.

[21] George E. Vaillant, *Aging Well: Surprising Guideposts to a Happier Life from the Landmark Harvard Study of Adult*

Development (New York: Little, Brown and Company, 2002), 246-48.

[22] Robert Waldinger, "What makes a good life? Lessons from the longest study on happiness," filmed November 2015 at TEDxBeaconStreet, video, 12:46, www.ted.com/talks/ robert_waldinger_what_makes_a_good_life_lessons_from_the_ longest_study_on_happiness.

[23] Marc E. Agronin, "It's Time to Rethink the Bucket-List Retirement," *The Wall Street Journal*, last modified March 21, 2016, www.wsj.com/articles/its-time-to-rethink-the-bucket-list-retirement-1458525877.

[24] Joan Chittister, *The Gift of Years: Growing Older Gracefully* (New York: BlueBridge, 2008), 36.

[25] Erik Erikson, *Childhood and Society* (New York: W. W. Norton & Company, 1963), quoted in Lewis Richmond, "Adulthood, Elderhood, Buddhahood: The Stages of a Spiritual Life," *The Huffington Post*, last modified September 9, 2011, www. huffingtonpost.com/lewis-richmond/adulthood-elderhood-buddh_b_891931.html.

[26] Marc Freedman, "Baby Boomers Plan to Keep Working but in a Different Way," *Next Avenue*, www.nextavenue.org/baby-boomers-plan-to-keep-working-but-in-a-different-way/.

[27] Nelson Mandela, "Nelson Mandela's speech at the launch of The Elders," *The Elders*, July 18, 2007, theelders.org/article/ nelson-mandelas-speech-launch-elders.

[28] Maia Szalavitz, "Friends With Benefits: Being Highly Social Cuts Dementia Risk by 70%," *Time*, May 2, 2011, healthland. time.com/2011/05/02/friends-with-benefits-being-highly-social-cuts-dementia-risk-by-70/.

[29] Katherine W. Phillips, "How Diversity Makes Us Smarter," *Scientific American*, October 1, 2014, www.scientificamerican. com/article/how-diversity-makes-us-smarter/.

[30] Barbara Bradley Hagerty, *Life Reimagined: The Science, Art, and Opportunity of Midlife* (New York: Riverhead Books, 2016), 95.

[31] Archana Singh and Nishi Misra, "Loneliness, depression and sociability in old age," *Industrial Psychiatry Journal* 18, no. 1, (2009): 51-55. doi:10.4103/0972-6748.57861.

[32] Atul Gawande, *Being Mortal: Medicine and What Matters in the End* (New York: Metropolitan Books, 2014), 126.

[33] Will Storr, "A Better Kind of Happiness," *The New Yorker*, July 7, 2016, www.newyorker.com/tech/elements/a-better-kind-of-happiness.

[34] P. L. Hill and N. A. Turiano, "Purpose in life as a predictor of mortality across adulthood," *Psychological Science* 25, no. 7, (2014): 1482-1486, doi: 10.1177/0956797614531799.

[35] Eric S. Kim, Victor J. Strecher, and Carol D. Ryff, "Purpose in life and use of preventive health care services," *Proceedings of the National Academy of Sciences of the United States of America* 111, no. 46 (2014): 16331-16336, www.ncbi.nlm.nih.gov/pmc/articles/PMC4246300/.

[36] George E. Vaillant, *Aging Well: Surprising Guideposts to a Happier Life from the Landmark Harvard Study of Adult Development* (New York: Little, Brown and Company, 2002), 224.

[37] Barbara Bradley Hagerty, *Life Reimagined: The Science, Art, and Opportunity of Midlife* (New York: Riverhead Books, 2016), 127-128.

[38] Daniel H. Pink, *Drive: The Surprising Truth About What Motivates Us* (New York: Penguin Publishing, 2009),135.

[39] P. L. Hill and N. A. Turiano, "Purpose in life as a predictor of mortality across adulthood," *Psychological Science* 25, no. 7, (2014): 1482-1486, doi: 10.1177/0956797614531799.

[40] Seneca, *On the Shortness of Life*, translated by C.D.N. Costa (New York: Penguin Books, 1997), quoted in Maria Popova, "The Shortness of Life: Seneca on Busyness and the Art of Living Wide Rather Than Living Long," *Brain Pickings*, September 1, 2014, www.brainpickings.org/2014/09/01/seneca-on-the-shortness-of-life/.

[41] Clayton M. Christensen, James Allworth, and Karen Dillon, *How Will You Measure Your Life?* (New York: HarperCollins, 2012).

[42] Mary Pipher, *Another Country: Navigating the Emotional Terrain of Our Elders* (New York: Riverhead Books, 1999), 245.

[43] Lewis Richmond, *Aging as a Spiritual Practice: A Contemplative Guide to Growing Older and Wiser* (New York: Gotham, 2012), 78-79.

[44] Lewis Richmond, "Vertical Time," YouTube video, 4:17, uploaded by Lewis Richmond, February 17, 2012, www.youtube.com/watch?v=fIkrpkq3Gf0.

[45] Ibid.

[46] George Kinder, "The Kinder Institute of Life Planning," *The Kinder Institute of Life Planning*, www.kinderinstitute.com.

[47] Dennis T. Jaffe, *Stewardship in Your Family Enterprise: Developing Responsible Family Leadership Across Generations* (Ross, CA: Pioneer Imprints, 2014), 218-219.

[48] Roberta K. Taylor and Dorian Mintzer, *The Couple's Retirement Puzzle: 10 Must-Have Conversations for Creating an Amazing New Life Together* (Naperville, IL: Sourcebooks, 2014), xxviii-xix.

[49] Lewis Richmond, *Aging as a Spiritual Practice: A Contemplative Guide to Growing Older and Wiser* (New York: Gotham, 2012), 11.

[50] "Discoveries of the American Legacies White Paper 2005," *The Allianz Life Insurance Co. of America*, 2005, www.allianzlife.com/-/media/files/allianz/documents/ent_120_n.pdf?la=en&hash=58FDB5A89AA791C6AAB30DFBF9044893 34367594.

[51] Beth Kurylo and Elaine Justice, "Family Meals, Stories Boost Child Confidence, Say Emory Researchers," *Emory University*, October 12, 2005, www.emory.edu/news/Releases/familymeals1129128206.html.

[52] Elaine Reese, "What Kids Learn From Hearing Family Stories," *The Atlantic*, December 9, 2013, www.theatlantic.com/education/archive/2013/12/what-kids-learn-from-hearing-family-stories/282075/.

[53] "Performance & Impact," *StoryCorps*, storycorps.org/performance-impact/.

[54] Marc E. Agronin, *How We Age: A Doctor's Journey into the Heart of Growing Old* (Cambridge, MA: Da Capo Press, 2011), 149.

[55] Elizabeth Arnold, *Creating the Good Will: The Most Comprehensive Guide to Both the Financial and Emotional Sides of Passing on Your Legacy* (New York: Portfolio, 2005), 5.

[56] Andrew Weil, *Healthy Aging: A Lifelong Guide to Your Physical and Spiritual Well-Being* (New York: Knopf, 2005), 290.

[57] Tovia Smith, "Ethical Wills," recorded segment of NPR's *Morning Edition*, December 21, 2001, www.npr.org/templates/story/story.php?storyId=1135121.

[58] David Solie, *How to Say It to Seniors: Closing the Communication Gap with Our Elders* (New York: Prentice Hall Press, 2004), 44-45.

[59] Atul Gawande, *Being Mortal: Medicine and What Matters in the End* (New York: Metropolitan Books, 2014), 105.

[60] Roger Landry, *Live Long, Die Short: A Guide to Authentic Health and Successful Aging* (Austin, TX: Greenleaf Book Group, 2014), 216.

[61] "The Search for Alzheimer's Causes and Risk Factors," *Alzheimer's Association*, accessed July 10, 2017, www.alz.org/ research/science/alzheimers_disease_causes.asp.

[62] Sherwin B. Nuland, *The Art of Aging: A Doctor's Prescription for Well-Being* (New York: Random House, 2007), 227.

[63] Sogyal Rinpoche, *The Tibetan Book of Living and Dying* eds. Patrick Gaffney and Andrew Harvey (San Francisco: HarperSanFrancisco, 1998), 16.

[64] "Where do Americans die?" *Stanford School of Medicine*, April 20, 2013, https://palliative.stanford.edu/home-hospice-home-care-of-the-dying-patient/where-do-americans-die.

[65] "The Conversation Project," *The Conversation Project*, accessed October 13, 2016, theconversationproject.org.

[66] Sogyal Rinpoche, *The Tibetan Book of Living and Dying* eds. Patrick Gaffney and Andrew Harvey (San Francisco: HarperSanFrancisco, 1998), 16.

[67] Oliver Sacks, *Gratitude* (New York: Knopf, 2015), 18.

[68] Ibid., 45.

[69] Ann Neumann, *The Good Death: An Exploration of Dying in America* (Boston: Beacon Press, 2016), 210.

[70] Vyjeyanthi S. Periyakoil, Eric Neri, and Helena Kraemer, "No Easy Talk: A Mixed Methods Study of Doctor Reported Barriers to Conducting Effective End-of-Life Conversations with Diverse Patients," *PLOS ONE* 10, no. 4 (2015), journals.plos.org/ plosone/article?id=10.1371/journal.pone.0122321.

71 "Serious Illness Conversation Guide," *Ariadne Labs*, PDF, last modified May 22, 2015, https://www.ariadnelabs.org/wp-content/uploads/sites/2/2017/05/SI-CG-2017-04-21_FINAL. pdf.

72 Andrew Solomon, "'The Good Death,' 'When Breath Becomes Air' and More," *The New York Times*, February 8, 2016, www.nytimes.com/2016/02/14/books/review/the-good-death-when-breath-becomes-air-and-more.html.

73 "'You've got to find what you love,' Jobs says," *Stanford News*, Stanford University, June 14, 2005, news.stanford. edu/2005/06/14/jobs-061505/.

74 Dennis Thompson, "More People Choosing Hospice at Life's End," *U.S. News & World Report*, January 28, 2011, https://health.usnews.com/health-news/managing-your-healthcare/healthcare/articles/2011/01/28/more-people-choosing-hospice-at-lifes-end.

75 Atul Gawande, *Being Mortal: Medicine and What Matters in the End* (New York: Metropolitan Books, 2014), 155.

76 Margaret Hathaway, "Death on the Farm," *Taproot Magazine*, Issue 17, March 2016.

77 Ann Neumann, *The Good Death: An Exploration of Dying in America* (Boston: Beacon Press, 2016), 1-5.

78 Sarah Putnam, "THE CONVERSATION PROJECT: I thought we had done it right," Vimeo video, 3:50, May 11, 2011, https://vimeo.com/23600823.

[79] Sogyal Rinpoche, *The Tibetan Book of Living and Dying* eds. Patrick Gaffney and Andrew Harvey (San Francisco: HarperSanFrancisco, 1998), 10.

[80] Atul Gawande, *Being Mortal: Medicine and What Matters in the End* (New York: Metropolitan Books, 2014), 243.

[81] Soygal Rinpoche, *The Tibetan Book of Living and Dying* eds. Patrick Gaffney and Andrew Harvey (San Francisco: HarperSanFrancisco, 1998), ix.

Notes

....

....

....

....

....

....

....

....

....

....

....

....

....

....

....

NOTES

NOTES